Regulatory Governance of the Rail Sector in Mexico

This work is published under the responsibility of the Secretary-General of the OECD. The opinions expressed and arguments employed herein do not necessarily reflect the official views of OECD member countries.

This document, as well as any data and map included herein, are without prejudice to the status of or sovereignty over any territory, to the delimitation of international frontiers and boundaries and to the name of any territory, city or area.

The statistical data for Israel are supplied by and under the responsibility of the relevant Israeli authorities. The use of such data by the OECD is without prejudice to the status of the Golan Heights, East Jerusalem and Israeli settlements in the West Bank under the terms of international law.

Please cite this publication as:
OECD (2020), *Regulatory Governance of the Rail Sector in Mexico*, OECD Publishing, Paris, *https://doi.org/10.1787/c21203ee-en*.

ISBN 978-92-82-11674-6 (print)
ISBN 978-92-82-18992-4 (pdf)

Photo credits: Cover © ayax/Shutterstock.com.

Corrigenda to publications may be found on line at: *www.oecd.org/about/publishing/corrigenda.htm*.
© OECD 2020

The use of this work, whether digital or print, is governed by the Terms and Conditions to be found at *http://www.oecd.org/termsandconditions*.

Foreword

Regulations play a fundamental role in the performance of an industry. They can facilitate -- or restrict -- the entry of new companies to a given market, and they can either stifle or promote innovation. While regulations are supposed to pursue a legitimate interest such as protecting consumers, workers and the environment, they may fail to achieve these objectives, and instead create unnecessary burdens on businesses and citizens. Therefore, regulations need to be reviewed and revised continually in order to ensure that they are "fit-for-purpose".

In Mexico, as in any country, the rail system can be a catalyst of economic activity by transporting inputs for production, distributing intermediate and consumer goods, and allowing people to travel to their workplace or leisure activities. To ensure the system can fulfil this potential, the Mexican government asked OECD to review the elements that define the regulatory governance of its rail sector, including the regulatory framework, the design and attributions of the regulatory oversight agency, and the way stakeholders of the rail system interact.

This report describes the series of structural reforms that the Mexican rail sector has undergone in the past 25 years. A major change was the shift from a publicly run rail service to a rail system under private concessions. More recently, the Regulatory Agency of Rail Transport was established as the sector's oversight body. These reforms were accompanied by an aggregated growth of 141% in the amount of cargo transported by the Mexican rail system: from 1995 to 2017, it increased from 52 million to 127 million tonnes.

Drawing on the OECD Recommendation on Regulatory Policy and Governance, the report also provides an assessment of the regulatory governance of the rail sector in Mexico, and offers recommendations to continue the reform efforts. It suggests ways to strengthen the capacities of the Regulatory Agency of Rail Transport to issue cost-effective regulations, and more effectively enforce existing rules. It also identifies gaps in the implementation and coverage of the current regulatory framework, such as in the framework related to trackage rights – the ability to use other companies' rail network – and methodologies to define fares.

The report also recommends that the Mexican government starts working on its medium-term vision of the rail system, considering that the exclusivity rights of most of the current concessions will expire in the next five to seven years. This report provides guidance on elements to consider when defining this new vision.

Acknowledgements

The current report was led by Manuel Flores Romero, Co-ordinator of the OECD programme on regulatory policy in Latin America of the OECD Regulatory Policy Division; and by Stephen Perkins, Head of Research and Policy of the International Transport Forum (ITF). The report was co-ordinated under the leadership of Nick Malyshev, Head of the Regulatory Policy Division and Marcos Bonturi, Director of Public Governance. The team received invaluable comments by the *peer reviewer*, Mr. Russell Pittman from the Department of Justice of the United States. The main authors are Stephen Perkins from the ITF, Andres Blancas, Gloriana Madrigal, Erik Perez and Manuel Flores Romero from the OECD Regulatory Policy Division. Significant contributions were received from Andrea Uhrhammer, Klas Klaas, and Marcos Bonturi. Claudia Paupe and Anna Kanjovski lent administrative and organisation support. Jennifer Stein co-ordinated the editorial process.

The review is based on information collected through a questionnaire in June 2018. The review team also held meetings in Mexico City in July and October 2018, with a wide range of stakeholders, including government officials from several ministries and government agencies, representatives from the academia and business community, and experts in regulatory and rail topics.

A draft of the key findings of the review was discussed in a lunchtime session with transport regulators at the OECD Network of Economic Regulators in April 2019. Thanks are extended to all members for their input and comments.

The OECD thanks the Ministry of Communications and Transport and the Regulatory Agency of Rail Transport (ARTF), in particular Mr. Alejandro Alvarez, Head of the ARFT and Gabriela Ignacio, Director of Internal Projects.

The OECD also thanks Mr. Benjamín Aleman, former Head of the ARTF and his team: Francisco Vargas, Oscar Cortes, and Estanislao Sandoval. Special thanks to Yuriria Mascott, former Deputy Minister of Transport.

Valuable information was provided by the teams of Regulated Markets, the Investigative Authority and the Legal Affairs Unit of the Federal Commission of Economic Competition (COFECE). The OECD thanks specially Octavio Gutierrez, Andrea Gamboa, Andrea Latapie and Myrna Mustieles for their comments and useful insights.

The comments and experience from stakeholders of the private sector represented a useful input for this review. The OECD appreciates the participation of Francisco Fabila and Edgar Aguileta from Kansas City Southern Mexico; Carlos Median and Jose Luis Perez form the Isthmus of Tehuantepec Rail; Francisco Jurado and Lourdes Aranda from Ferromex; Erich Wetzel from FERROVALLE and Carlos Anaya form the Sub-urban Rail.

The OECD recognises the insights offered by Mr. Carlos Mier y Terán and Roberto Vargas Molina from Mexico's National Bank for Public Services and Construction (Banobras). In addition, the OECD thanks Mr. Guillermo Lecona from the Ministry of Finance (SHCP) for his useful comments.

The OECD also thanks Francisco Kim and Leonardo Gomez from Mexico's National Association of Private Transportation (ANTP); Iker Casillas from the Mexican Rail Association (AMF); Roberto Aguerrebere and Carmen Martinez from then Mexican Institute of Transport (IMT).

Finally, the OECD thanks Fernando Bueno, Jose Valente, Fatima Guzman, Eduardo Bravo and Jessica Chaparro from the Ministry of Transport and Communications. Also, comments were received from Victor Silva, Sandra Hernández and Jorge Hernández from the General Direction of Rail and Multimodal Rail Transport.

Table of contents

Acronyms and abbreviations — 9

Legal instruments that affect rail services in Mexico — 11

Executive summary — 12

1 Assessment and recommendations — 14
    Assessment on rail regulation — 15
    Assessment on governance of the Regulatory Agency of Rail Transport — 21
    Recommendations related to rail regulation — 31
    Recommendations on governance — 33
    Notes — 37
    References — 37

2 Performance of the rail sector of Mexico — 39
    Industry analysis — 40
    Spatial analysis — 48
    International Comparison — 54
    References — 57

3 State of play and reforms of the rail sector of Mexico — 58
    Development of railways from the 19th century to 1994 — 59
    1995 Law on the Regulation of Rail Services and Mexico's Railway Concessions — 60
    2015 Amendments to the Law and Establishment of the Regulatory Agency for Rail Transport — 70
    Additional amendments to the Law on the Regulation of Rail Services — 73
    International practice on regulation and governance of the rail sector — 74
    References — 82

4 Internal governance of the Regulatory Agency for Rail Transport — 86
    Role clarity — 87
    Preventing undue influence and maintaining trust — 89
    Decision making and government body structure for independent regulators — 90
    Accountability and transparency — 92
    Stakeholder engagement — 93
    Funding — 93
    Performance evaluation — 94
    References — 95

Glossary and definitions — 96

Tables

Table 1.1. Characteristics and challenges of the Mexican Law of Regulatory Improvement	20
Table 1.2. Rail's Health and Safety Regulation levy scheme	28
Table 2.1. Freight and passenger by transportation mode	40
Table 2.2. Freight transportation by year and mode	41
Table 2.3. Freight transport by mode	42
Table 2.4. Rail freight transportation in Mexico	45
Table 2.5. Rail freight transportation by group product, in tonnes	47
Table 2.6. Rail freight transportation by group of product	47
Table 2.7. Distribution of the cargo remitted by concessionaires and assignees in Mexico	48
Table 2.8. Freight according to the type of traffic in Mexico	50
Table 2.9. Main freight nodes for local traffic in Mexico	51
Table 2.10. Interlineal sent traffic in Mexico	52
Table 2.11. Interlineal traffic in transit in Mexico	54
Table 3.1. Sale prices for the main concessions in Mexico	63
Table 3.2. Concession periods for freight rail transportation in Mexico	65
Table 3.3. Mandatory trackage rights assigned and received in concession titles in Mexico	67
Table 3.4. Mandatory trackage and haulage rights included in the concession titles in Mexico	67
Table 3.5. Example of trackage and haulage rights in concession titles in Mexico: North-Pacific Concession	69
Table 3.6. Network Rail Income in England and Wales	72
Table 4.1. Selected functions of the ARTF	88

Figures

Figure 1.1. Total income from ORR's rail and roads functions	28
Figure 2.1. Evolution of the freight transport	41
Figure 2.2. Investment by main rail concessionaires in Mexico	43
Figure 2.3. Average growth in gross domestic product (GDP) of the freight transport in Mexico between 1994 and 2017	44
Figure 2.4. Year to year growth in GDP of the freight transport in Mexico between 1994 and 2017	44
Figure 2.5. Freight moved by rail	45
Figure 2.6. Average tariffs of rail freight	46
Figure 2.7. Cargo distribution of freight rail by destination in Mexico	49
Figure 2.8. Share of international rail cargo by international crossing and port in Mexico	50
Figure 2.9. Rail lines density	55
Figure 2.10. Rail tonne-km vs GDP	56
Figure 2.11. Rail infrastructure investment as % of GDP	57
Figure 3.1. The initial concession structure in Mexico	63
Figure 3.2. Principle mandatory trackage rights specified in concession titles	64
Figure 3.3. Mexico's rail concessions and short lines in 2018	65
Figure 3.4. International comparisons of rail share of rail vs truck ton-km (%)	74
Figure 3.5. Rail commodity distribution in North America	75
Figure 3.6. U.S. freight railway tariff structure with revenue masked	76

Boxes

Box 1.1. The one-in, x-out practice in OECD countries and in Mexico	18
Box 1.2. The role clarity principle in regulator: country example	22
Box 1.3. Preventing undue influence and maintain trust: some country examples	23
Box 1.4. Decision-making and government body structure for economic regulators: country examples	24
Box 1.5. Accountability and transparency in the UK Office of Rail and Road (ORR)	25
Box 1.6. Stakeholder Engagement: Corporate strategy and annual forward work programme of OFGEM in the United Kingdom	26
Box 1.7. Funding in the UK's Office of Rail and Road	28
Box 1.8. Italian Regulatory Authority for Electricity, Gas and Water performance indicators & assessment framework	29

Box 1.9. Activities carried out to enhance the performance of the railway system by the ARTF 2018-2024 administration 32
Box 1.10. Activities carried out to enhance the performance of the inspections by the ARTF 2018-2024 administration 34
Box 1.11. Activities carried out to boost the stakeholder engagement practices by the ARTF 2018-2024 administration 36
Box 3.1. Short summary of TRB conclusions on modernising US freight rail regulation 78

Acronyms and abbreviations

ACCC	Australian Competition and Consumer Commission
Admicarga	Administrator of the short line Tijuana Tecate (*Administradora de la vía corta Tijuana Tecate*)
AEEGSI	Italian Regulatory Authority for Electricity, Gas and Water (*Autorità per l'Energia Elettrica, il Gas e il Sistema Idrico*)
AMF	Mexican Rail Association (*Asociación Mexicana de Ferrocarriles*)
ANTP	National Association of Private Transportation (*Asociación Nacional de Transporte Privado*)
ARCEP	Regulatory Authority of the Electronic Communications and Mail (*Autorité de Régulation des Communications Électroniques et des Postes*)
ARTF	Regulatory Agency of Rail Transport (*Agencia Reguladora del Transporte Ferroviario*)
BANOBRAS	Mexico's National Bank for Public Construction (*Banco Nacional de Obras y Servicios Públicos*)
BNetzA	Federal Network Agency (*Bundesnetzagentur*)
CAF	Construction and Ancillary of Railways (*Construcciones y Auxiliar de Ferrocarriles S.A*).
CCNN	National Advisory Committees for Standardisation
Chepe	Rail Chihuahua-Pacifico (*Ferrocarril Chihuahua-Pacífico*)
CLR	Competitive Line Rate
CN	Canadian National
CNMC	National Market and Competition Commission (*Comisión Nacional de los Mercados y la Competencia*)
COAGEC	Council of Australian Governments Energy Council
COFECE	Federal Commission of Economic Competition (*Comisión Federal de Competencia Económica*)
COFEMER	Federal Regulatory Commission (*Comisión Federal de Mejora Regulatoria*)
CONAMER	National Commission of Regulatory Improvement (*Comisión Nacional de Mejora Regulatoria*)
CP	Canadian Pacific
CRE	Energy Regulatory Commission (*Comisión Reguladora de la Energía*)
CTA	Canadian Transportation Agency
CTA	Canada Transportation Act
Defra	Department of Environment, Food, and Rural Affairs
DGDFM	General Direction of Rail and Multimodal Transport Development (*Dirección General de Desarrollo Ferroviario y Multimodal*)
DOF	Official Gazzette of the Federation (*Diario Oficial de la Federación*)
ERSAR	Water and Wastes Services Regulation Authority (*Entidade Reguladora dos Serviços de Águas e Resíduos*)
FCCM	Rail Company Chiapas-Mayab (*Compañía de Ferrocarriles Chiapas-Mayab*)

FdelP	Pacific Railway (*Ferrocarril del Pacífico*)
Ferromex	Mexican Railways company (*Ferrocarriles Mexicanos*)
Ferrovalle	Mexico Valley Railroad and Terminal (*Ferrocarril y Terminal del Valle de México*)
FIT	Isthmus of Tehuantepec Rail (*Ferrocarril del Istmo de Tehuantepec*)
FNM	National Railways of Mexico (*Ferrocarriles Nacionales de Mexico*)
GDP	Gross domestic product
HHI	Herfindahl-Hirschman Index
ICC	Interstate Commerce Commission
IFT	Federal Institute of Telecommunications (*Instituto Federal de Telecomunicaciones*)
IMT	Mexican Institute of Transport (*Instituto Mexicano del Transporte*)
IT	Information Technology
ITF	International Transport Forum
KCSM	Kansas City Southern Mexico
LFCD	Coahuila-Durango Line (*Línea Coahuila-Durango*)
LRSF	Law on the Regulation of Rail Services (*Ley Reglamentaria del Servicio Ferroviario*)
NAO	National Audit Office
NdeM	Nationals of Mexico (*Nacionales de México*)
NEB	National Energy Board
Nkom	Norwegian Communications Authority
Ofgem	Office of Gas and Electricity Markets
Ofwat	Water Services Regulation Authority
ORR	Office of Rail and Road, United Kingdoms
PUC	Public Utilities Commission
RIA	Regulatory impact assessment
SCT	Ministry of Communications and Transport (*Secretaría de Comunicaciones y Transporte*)
SFP	Ministry of Public Administration (*Secretaría de la Función Pública*)
SHCP	Ministry of Finance (*Secretaría de Hacienda y Crédito Público*)
SoE	Statement of Expectations
SoI	Statement of Intent
STB	Surface Transport Board
TFM	Mexican Railway Transportation (*Transportación Ferroviaria Mexicana*)
TFVM	Ferrocarril y Terminal Ferroviaria del Valle de México
TMM	Mexican Maritime Transportation (*Transportación Marítima Mexicana*)
TRB	Transportation Research Board

Legal instruments that affect rail services in Mexico

Legal Instrument	Name in Spanish	Date of Publication	Web link
Law on the Regulation of Rail Services	*Ley Reglamentaria del Servicio Ferroviario*	Last reform 24-04-2018	http://www.diputados.gob.mx/LeyesBiblio/pdf/209_240418.pdf
Bylaw on Rail Services	*Reglamento del Servicio Ferroviario*	Last reform 18-08-2016	https://www.dof.gob.mx/nota_detalle.php?codigo=5448475&fecha=18/08/2016
Federal Law on Metrology and Standardisation	*Ley Federal sobre Metrología y Normalización*	Last reform 15-06-2018	http://www.diputados.gob.mx/LeyesBiblio/pdf/130_150618.pdf
General Law for Regulatory Improvement	*Ley General de Mejora Regulatoria*		
Decree SCT 26-01-2015, modifying the Law on the Regulation of Rail Services for the creation of the ARTF	*Decreto SCT 26-01-2015, modificación de la Ley Reglamentaria del Servicio Ferroviario para la creación de la ARTF*	26-01-2015	http://dof.gob.mx/nota_detalle.php?codigo=5379469&fecha=26/01/2015
Decree SCT 18-08-2016, modification of the internal bylaw of the SCT for the delimitation of the duties of the General Directorate for Rail and Multimodal Development	*Decreto SCT 18-08-2016, modificación del reglamento interior de la SCT para la delimitación de funciones de la Dirección General de Desarrollo Ferroviario y Multimodal*	18-08-2016	https://www.dof.gob.mx/nota_detalle.php?codigo=5448474&fecha=18/08/2016

Executive summary

In 1995, the government reformed Mexico's railways by statute through the Law on the Regulation of Rail Services. This provided for the publicly run rail network to be divided into a small number of exclusive, vertically integrated private freight railway concessions. The 1995 railway reforms achieved a complete turnaround in the performance of the Mexican railway sector. GDP in rail freight transport grew on average 4.1% per year from 1995-2017, outperforming all other modes of transport.

After a series of amendments to the 1995 Law, the Regulatory Agency for Rail Transport (ARTF) was created, with the primary objective of enhancing the government's capacity for implementing regulations concerning trackage rights and tariff protection, among others.

Main assessment

- Strengthening regulatory capacity through the establishment of the ARTF was an essential step in fostering development of a safe, efficient and competitive rail system in Mexico. ARTF has made consistent progress in filling the gaps in the regulatory capacity required to ensure implementation of the Law on the Regulation of Rail Services. However, many challenges still need to be addressed, including budgeting, regulatory, and governance issues, in order to achieve full implementation of the legal provisions.
- Nevertheless, the time taken to implement some of the main trackage rights mandated in the concession agreements for interconnection and competition suggests inadequate regulatory capacity to enforce the law.
- There is a gap in the regulation to define the process and methodology for determining tariffs when two concession holders do not reach agreement in interconnection services, or for captive shippers in the absence of competition.
- The end of exclusive use of their networks in many concessions poses challenges to competition and regulatory authorities, with implications for the future of the rail system in Mexico.
- The objectives, functions, attributions and duties of the ARTF are scattered between the Law on the Regulation of Rail Services and the decree of creation of the ARTF and are concentrated in its organisational manual. Currently, regulatory and promotion duties are combined, which blurs the role of the agency.
- The ARFT regularly publishes information on safety and other indicators in the rail sector; however, this information is limited in scope. The agency does not currently promote wider public accountability besides reporting to the Ministry of Communications and Transport and the Ministry of Finance.
- The ARTF has limitations on its ability to acquire the funding it needs to accomplish the objectives and functions stated in the legal framework.

Main recommendations

- The ARTF may wish to evaluate if and where the introduction of additional trackage rights could unlock significant gains in network-wide efficiency and competitiveness for Mexican industry without undermining the sustainability of the rail services provided already by the concessions. A good network model would be extremely useful in making these assessments and evaluations.
- In developing capacity to make the provisions for connectivity and competition in the law fully operational, ARTF could concentrate on establishing the basis for tariff regulation for both captive shippers and cases of failure to reach agreement on mandated trackage and haulage rights. Such charges will need to cover marginal costs, as stipulated in the Law. For captive shippers, a guideline for identifying abusive prices is needed.
- ARTF could also examine the availability of interline services and develop procedures for setting regulated tariffs where concessions fail to offer services.
- The Ministry of Communications and Transport and the Mexican government more broadly need to begin work on its vision for the railway system post 2027 without delay, as the investment cycle of railways is much longer than 9 years. ARTF's expert opinion could be sought in this regard.
- The regulatory framework that defines the role and functions of ARTF could be reviewed to strive for a reform that focus the Agency´s functions in regulatory roles, while allocating promotion duties to General Direction of Rail Development. In the short term, the ARTF could create a strategy document to define its priorities between its current regulatory and promotion duties.
- An assessment of the inspection duties of the ARTF would help define the resources needed to discharge this function properly. Short- and long-term strategies for complying with these duties should be defined, considering formal co-operation agreements with the Ministry of Communications and Transport's centres while ARTF acquires its own capacities.
- Guidelines and other regulatory instruments are needed to establish an effective sanctioning system.
- The Agency could consider establishing practices on accountability and transparency that go beyond its current obligations that derive from the national framework. For instance, the ARTF should improve the quantity and the quality of information it publishes on its web portal in user-friendly formats.
- In order to strengthen accountability and transparency practices, the ARTF could boost its reporting mechanisms by submitting yearly reports to Congress separately from the reporting of the Ministry of Communications and Transport. Proactive mechanisms could also be adopted to submit the report to other key stakeholders, such as industry association and sector experts, and seek their feedback.
- The Ministry of Communications and Transport, the Ministry of Finance and the ARTF could review the funding requirements of the agency in order to define the budget the agency needs to discharge its duties effectively. In this revision, consideration should be given to implementing the necessary reforms to allow ARTF to propose its budget autonomously and implement it independently within the limits set in the annual budget law for the calendar year. Additionally, these reforms could include provisions to give a portion of the fee currently charged to the regulated entities directly to ARTF.

1 Assessment and recommendations

This chapter presents the assessment and recommendations from this report. The first section contains the assessment, which is divided between findings related to rail regulation, and findings related to the governance of the Regulatory Agency of Rail Transport. For each finding, the corresponding arguments which led to the particular conclusion are developed. The second section contains the recommendations, which offer concrete proposals to address the afore-mentioned findings.

Assessment on rail regulation

1. *Strengthening regulatory capacity through the establishment of the Regulatory Agency of Rail Transport (ARTF) was an essential and overdue step in the approach to fostering development of a safe, efficient and competitive rail system in Mexico. ARTF has made consistent progress in filling the gap in the regulatory capacity required to ensure that the Law on the Regulation of Rail Services is implemented. However, many challenges remain including budgeting, regulatory, and governance issues, in order to aspire to a full implementation of the legal provisions.*

ARTF has implemented all of the short-term objectives set for it in the 2015 revisions to the Law on the Regulation of Rail Services. ARTF is focusing on ensuring the technical tools for execution of its mandate are in place. This includes the collection of detailed and accurate information on railroad revenues and costs as well as the ability of the agency staff to analyze and utilise such data. It includes updating the register of assets of the concessions and updating the technical requirements for inspection and maintenance of track. The latter has already made a significant improvement to ensuring safe operation of the system. Maintaining an updated register of surcharges on carriage rates is also important. Some traffic is extremely sensitive to these charges, and changes in the "discounts" applied by concession holders can have a major impact of the viability of traffic. It also includes the collection of accurate, verifiable information as to which trackage rights are currently being utilised, and the details of their usage.

However, budget restrictions have slowed progress, delaying recruitment of specialist staff and resulting in posts being filled by staff with additional duties in other areas of rail policy, diluting the resources available for regulation. Delays seem largely or entirely due to this underfunding, and management direction and planning has been effective in these constrained circumstances.

Additionally, there are gaps in the legislation which prevents action aimed at implementing the legal provisions fully, which has an impact in the development of rail services. These include issues on trackage rights, tariffs and competition issues, as well as challenges in the governance design of ARTF (discussed in detail below).

The delays and challenges mean that the full impact of the establishment of ARTF will not be apparent in the short term. Resourcing of the Agency should be strengthened to facilitate delivery on its mandate and any further reform should build on the successes achieved thus far through the interventions of ARTF rather than take a new direction.

2. *The time taken to implement some of the main trackage rights mandated in the concession agreements for interconnection and competition reflects inadequate regulatory capacity to enforce the law.*

The 1995 Law on the Regulation of Rail Services provides for the Ministry of Communications and Transport (SCT) to grant concessions to private companies to operate rail lines under conditions established by the Ministry and set out in the concession titles. Terms of access to rail infrastructure are established by the three instruments – the law, the bylaw and the concession title agreements – together. The concessions were designed to maximise the income produced by sale of the leases and therefore provided long periods of exclusive access to markets.

Specific trackage and haulage rights were provided for in the annexes to the concession agreements as an exception to the exclusivity granted to the concession holder. These trackage rights enable a concession holder to operate freight services over the tracks of the other concession. Some of these trackage and haulage rights included in the concession deeds were to provide for competition, most for more practical operational reasons. Most are limited to specific products, routes, slots and origin-destination pairs (excluding commercial service between intermediate points).

Some of the rights designed to promote interconnection were implemented without delay,[1] serving specific industry plants or connecting fragmented networks. However, there were cases of stalled negotiations between concessions on terms of use for many of the rights[2], and the use of other trackage rights has been problematic.

The concession holders are also allowed to use trackage rights on a voluntary basis to manage disruptions and congested sections of track (Regulation 107). However, there is generally no incentive for concessions to agree to terms on rights designed to facilitate competition, and their underlying interest is to preserve exclusive markets rather than compete for clients and undermine exclusivity.

The government also reserved the right in the titles to assign additional trackage rights for passenger trains. It also reserved the right to assign additional trackage and haulage rights for freight trains in the public interest – conditioned on the economic and technical feasibility from the point of view of the concession, the international traffic and on the basis of reciprocity. Now, no test of economic feasibility has been specified, and no awards on trackage or haulage rights have been made. These provisions are set out in Article 1.4.2 of the concession agreements.

The establishment of the ARTF helped alleviate some of the limited regulatory capacity by the Ministry of Transport and Communications (SCT) to enforce and promote the use of trackage rights, which has an impact in the promotion of development of rail services though more intense competition, although there are still operational, legislative and governance gaps, which are discussed next. Weak enforcement capacity to date suggests there is possibly an unexploited potential for improvement in efficiency and quality of service through development of competition within the current framework of the law.

Combined with an operational basis for tariff regulation (see below), the recent expiry of the 20 year period of exclusivity from trackage and haulage rights in concession agreements as an alternative protection for captive shippers to regulated tariffs may demand more private agreements regarding trackage and haulage rights, with recourse for shippers to ARTF should agreements prove elusive, hence the importance to strengthen regulatory capacity for the Agency.

> 3. *There is a gap in the regulation to define the process and methodology to determine tariffs when two concession holders do not reach agreement in interconnection services, or for captive shippers in the absence of competition*

The Law on the Regulation of Rail Services, as amended in 2015, has as its stated purpose "to regulate the construction, operation, exploitation, preservation and maintenance of railways and guarantee their interconnection … as well as to foster the conditions for competition in public rail transport services…". The law and the concession titles balance the basic freedom of concession holders to set tariffs freely and enjoy exclusive use of their networks with rights for concessions to compete between them using trackage rights in specified circumstances and provide protections for captive shippers from abusive tariffs.

In line with this thinking, the amended Law on the Regulation of Rail Services includes specific provisions in article 35 for the ARTF to set tariffs whenever two concession holders with interconnection services and associated trackage or haulage do not agree on establishing access rights and charges voluntarily, and in article 36 to establish mandatory trackage rights on specific routes when COFECE finds an absence of effective competition in a specific area.

However, currently, there is not an established official methodology and process for ARTF to establish access rights and charges where these are not agreed voluntarily. Furthermore, the law omits to specify what action a shipper might take if neither concession proposes a tariff or if the proposals are unacceptable, and no role is identified for the Agency (or for COFECE) in the absence of agreement.

Therefore, a gap in the law exists, because it fails to specify procedures to be followed when concessions fail to offer rates for interline services or offer only uncompetitive tariffs. A lack of regulatory capacity until the establishment of ARTF may also explain the absence of any instance of recourse to the provisions of the law to protect captive shippers through tariff regulation.

4. *The recent and forthcoming end of exclusivity to the use of their networks in many concessions poses challenges to competition and regulatory authorities, with implications on the future of the rail system in Mexico*

COFECE has undertaken a very thorough assessment of competition in markets involving interconnection between concession networks (COFECE, 2016[1]). Its preliminary assessment found widespread absence of effective competition, but ultimately it was deemed the evidence was insufficient to take action. The Law on the Regulation of Rail Services provides for ARTF to remedy specific instances of absence of effective competition. Should ARTF ask COFECE to examine specific markets where it expects to find a net overall benefit from intervention, with a narrower definition of the relevant market, COFECE could confirm a lack of effective competition if the provisions of the law are met, and the investigation of COFECE provides the necessary supporting evidence.

In this scenario where absence of effective competition is determined by COFECE, ARTF would have to act to ensure that trackage and haulage rights are awarded on the rail network under assessment, and that the corresponding tariffs are set.

COFECE (2016[1]) interprets that the capacity for ARTF to ensure the award of trackage rights in the absence of competition only applies once the 20-year period of exclusivity set in the concessions is over. Considering that in exclusivity periods in most of the concessions end in 9 years, an increase in the demand of functions and resources of the ARTF is warranted. This puts additional pressure to issue the necessary regulatory framework for an effective operation of the Agency, and to address the budgetary and governance challenges discussed below.

The government could make more systematic changes to the competition framework across the network, but during the periods of exclusivity awarded in the concession titles this may require compensation to be paid to the concession holders to the extent that the new arrangements could reduce the value of the concessions.

Additionally, SCT and the government more broadly needs to begin work on its vision for the railway system post 2027 without delay, as the investment cycle of railways is much longer than 9 years. In this vision, a balance between exclusivity and intramodal as well as intermodal competition should be sought.

5. *A key objective of the Agency is to issue regulation – notably safety and technical regulation. For the former, the ARTF follows good regulatory practices established by the National Commission on Regulatory Improvement (CONAMER); for the latter, the ARTF recently established a National Advisory Committee for Standardisation (CCNN) as mandated by the Federal Metrology and Standardisation Law. However, there is not a forward planning agenda to prioritise on the regulation to be issued, which is also affected by the 'one-in, one-out' rule established to control de flows of regulation by the Mexican government.*

According to the organisation manual, one of ARTF's key objectives is the issuance of subordinate regulation, including technical regulation. So far, prioritisation to issue regulation by the ARTF is on lagging issues as opposed to a structured forward planning agenda constructed from criteria discussed with stakeholders, i.e. government agencies, regulated entities, experts or public in general. This affects the capacity of the ARTF to focus resources on the most needed regulation.

Additionally, Mexico recently introduced a new General Law for Regulatory Improvement that obliges regulatory agencies to a "one-in, x-out" principle (see Box 1.1). Namely, if a regulation is to be issued, the compliance costs it generates need to be stricken from another existing regulation. This rule has limited the capacity of the ARTF to issue regulation as it lacks a stock of regulations to be eliminated to comply with the rule.

> ### Box 1.1. The one-in, x-out practice in OECD countries and in Mexico
>
> **What is the one-in x-out practice?**
>
> A one-in, x-out rule is a policy to offset potential burdens created by new regulations, by reducing or eliminating current ones. Thus, the practice requires eliminating an x number of regulations in order to release any new. In practice, the one-in, x-out rule can be implemented in several ways. For example, eliminating rule by rule or by offsetting equivalent negative impacts (more like a cost-in, cost-out rule) instead of a specific number of regulations.
>
> The most commonly rationale for limiting regulatory costs relies in the negative correlation between such costs (measured as a proportion of gross the domestic product) and the economic performance in terms of economic and employment growth
>
> **Summary of practices in OECD countries**
>
> The offsetting approach has its roots in setting net quantitative targets for reducing administrative costs. This was pioneered in the Netherlands in the 1990s with the introduction of the Standard Cost Model – a method to quantify administrative burdens in monetary terms. The United Kingdom was the first OECD country to formalise a One-In, One-Out approach in 2011. Canada, Spain and Germany, followed the rule in 2012, 2013 and 2015, respectively. More recently, Korea, USA, Mexico and France introduced their versions of regulatory offsetting. Australia implemented the rule and later abandoned it. Finland has just completed a pilot project testing a one-in, one-out policy.
>
> **United States:** Agencies shall revise or repeal two existing regulations for every new federal regulation that imposes costs. The rule asks to ensure that the total incremental regulatory costs of all new regulations offset by revised or repealed regulations, should be no greater than zero. The US approach takes into account all opportunity costs to society, direct or indirect – according to the Office of Management and Budget the opportunity costs is the appropriate concept for valuing both benefits and costs. The approach makes the process better connected to the regulatory impact assessment process; however, calculating all opportunity costs might be time-consuming, costly and dependant on the appropriate (econometrical) models.
>
> **Canada:** The One for One rule was introduced in April 2012 based on the Red Tape Reduction Commission's Recommendation Report. The rule requires offsetting new direct administrative burdens on business imposed for any regulatory change, by removing an equal amount of burdens from the stock of regulations. The rule also entails removing an existing regulation every time a new enacted rule imposes new administrative burdens on business.
>
> **France:** A moratorium established in 2013 for new regulations was similar to the One for One, in which departments are required to both: offset the increase in costs to businesses and to remove or simplify an existing regulation when other is enacted. The difference relied in the local governments and citizens' costs, which were also considered. In 2017, the rule was extended into the two-for-one policy with the intent to impose greater control on the regulatory flow of texts, as the original approach did not achieve the desired results.
>
> **United Kingdom:** The One-In, One-Out approach was established in 2011. The programme was deemed highly successful and the Government decided to double the offsetting targets by introducing the One-In, Two-Out. In 2015 the approach was even strengthened and every pound in cost created by

any new regulation had to be offset by a reduction of 3 pounds, creating the One-In, Three Out. The rule was a tool to achieve the Business Impact Target of reducing regulatory costs for businesses by 10 billion GBP for five years until the end in 2020. Regulatory offsetting was replaced in 2017 with a focus on promoting more efficient regulation, founded on high-quality evidence and supporting by transparency and accountability for costs and benefits.

Challenges

The rule one-in, x-out has many challenges in their implementation. Here some of the most relevant:

- The proper identification of costs and benefits, which can be direct or indirect. The measurement of costs is also a relevant challenge as it is time consuming and costly.
- Simple rules do not fit all cases. In new institutions and rising or developing industries there may be a need to create regulation to control risks, instead of reduce burdens. Thus, offsetting is not a real option and there is a need to establish special situations.
- The offsetting rule may be a burden by itself if there is no training, transparency and clear rules.
- Efforts analysing the potential effects of the x-out rule may have an impact on the current resources used in the development of the Regulatory Impact Assessment.

The one-in one-out rule in Mexico

In March of 2017, the Federal Government published in the Official Gazette, a decree with the guidelines to implement the one-in, two-out rule, for any entity of the federal administration that pretends to issue administrative acts, according to the Federal Law of Administrative Procedures – specifically under the scope of the Article 69-H regarding compliance costs. The rule focused on preventing the issuing of administrative acts, if they were to create compliance costs – except for some exemptions. These include emergencies, obligations from primary laws, international commitments, recurrent regulations, net positive benefits, etc.

The decree indicated that, if an entity sought to publish an administrative act, it must include within the draft project, two regulations that will be dropped from the same sector – Article 5. Then, the COFEMER (now CONAMER) could verify a net reduction of compliance costs. According to the COFEMER, 73 regulatory drafts were subject to the decree between March 9 and October 31 of 2017, resulting in cost savings equivalent to MXN 31 347.94 million – the costs generated by the new regulations summed up 1 758.06 million of pesos and the net reduction of costs was 29 589.88 million (COFEMER, 2017[2]).

In May 18 of 2018, the government published the current General Law of Regulatory Improvement. The law states that if any regulation creates compliance costs, the draft project must include the regulatory obligations or acts that must be abrogated to compensate the new burden. Thus, the new rule in Mexico is from the type cost-in, cost-out.

In Mexico, the *Comisión Nacional de Mejora Regulatoria* (CONAMER) is responsible for overseeing the implementation of the current one-in, one-out rule, and for this purpose monitors the offsetting of compliance costs for individuals following the introduction of a new regulation.

As in the decree, the law resumes the exceptions of the implementation of the one-in, one-out. However, there are no guidelines to properly adopt the rule and standardise practices. Also, there are no considerations for cases as new institutions and new or non-updated regulations across sectors.

Table 1.1. Characteristics and challenges of the Mexican Law of Regulatory Improvement

Concept	Features	Challenge
One-in, one-out	Cost offsetting	Timing and cost in measuring.
Guidelines	No guidelines	No clauses for new institutions and rising industries.
Implementation plan	No implementation plan	There are no evidence of training and transparency efforts. Misconception of the tool. Trade-offs between human resources in the adoption of the tool.
Subordinate regulation	No by-laws	Uncertainty about specific cases and implementation of the tool.

Source: (Trnka and Thuerer, 2019[3]), "One-In, X-Out: Regulatory offsetting in selected OECD countries", OECD Regulatory Policy Working Papers, No. 11, Paris, https://doi.org/10.1787/67d71764-en.

Furthermore, the one-in, one-out principle lacks of guidelines to implement the policy in standard basis and with complete certainty. The rule up to now is only indicated as an obligation to compensate for new regulation but with few exemptions, it does not take into account situations of urgency, new institutions, etc.

The absence of a forward planning agenda to issue regulation (see below) along with the one in, one-out affects the capacity of the ARTF to address regulatory issues of prominence.

6. *The ARTF and the General Direction of Rail Development of the SCT (DGDFM) are formally separated, but still share personnel, activities, administrative procedures and functions. In the operation, the agency and the General Direction have not defined what information belongs to each entity and personnel may play different roles within the ARTF and the general direction simultaneously.*

The ARTF was granted with specific regulatory capacities by the law, but the SCT, the Ministry of Finance (SHCP) and the Ministry of Public Administration (SFP) have not finished yet the administrative arrangements to transfer all designated personnel to the agency. The ARTF must have 67 officials, most of them stemming from the DGDFM. Nonetheless, after two years, the ARTF has 18 officials and the allocation of the other 49 is still pending. Nowadays, the ARTF has regulatory responsibilities that cannot formally develop as the personnel is still in the DGDFM.

Additionally, some staff pending to be transferred has roles and functions within the DGDFM that should be performed by the ARTF, and it is not clear whether these activities will also be transferred along with the personnel to ARTF, or will remain in the DGDFM.

There is crucial information that ARTF still lacks and requires to perform its functions properly. For instance, the ARTF does not have a complete copy of the rail concessions and the DGDFM fails to provide it. In this sense, the ARTF turns to the concession holders in order to get some information.

On the other hand, clear allocation of financial resources and separated functions between public officials are pending issues in both the DGDFM and the ARTF. For instance, personnel in charge of the inspection process receive their travel allowance from the SCT while supervision in fact comes from the ARTF. This situation arises, as the ARTF lacks of proper and enough personnel to undertake an inspection process. For instance, the ARTF requires support from SCT to conduct an inspection process and the ARTF is the oversight body.

7. *The regulatory framework of rail in Mexico does not establish provisions for the participation of the ARTF in the concession process – being the SCT the sole responsible. The ARTF should participate in the process as they can provide non-binding opinions on regulatory matters. This is relevant because the ARTF is the agency that will interact with the regulated firms after concessions are granted.*

The SCT is the entity responsible for the concession granting process in the rail sector. The current law does not include the participation of the ARTF in such a process – even though they participate informally. However, a more systematic participation of the ARTF would be useful as it is the institution in charge of monitoring the behaviour of the regulated entities.

A concession process in which SCT and ARTF co-ordinate beforehand may avoid asymmetries of information and align expectations about the future participation of each party. Thus, a more efficient and effective implementation of the regulatory framework can be achieved.

Assessment on governance of the Regulatory Agency of Rail Transport

In a context where there is a constant expectation for quick and efficient policy results, establishing high-performing regulators is a relevant element to attain good regulatory outcomes. For this purpose, regulatory agencies should aim at establishing institutional arrangements and organisational structures that allow them to reach their objectives effectively and to address the challenges efficiently.

The *OECD Best Practice Principles for Regulatory Policy: The Governance of Regulators* sets forward seven principles for regulatory agencies to improve their performance (OECD, 2014[4]).

> 8. *Role clarity: the objectives, functions, attributions and duties of the ARTF are scattered between the Law on the Regulation of Rail Services and the decree of creation of the ARTF and are concentrated in its organisational manual. Currently, regulatory and promotion duties are combined, which blurs the role of the agency. Furthermore, the ARTF cannot undertake some regulatory duties due to the lack of institutional capacities and gaps in regulation. Additionally, after two years of existence, personnel and functions of the ARTF and the General Direction of Rail Development are still mixed and with overlapping functions.*

The ARTF was established on August 2016 as a deconcentrated body attached to the SCT. According to the decree of creation, the agency is responsible for overseeing three main aspects of rail transportation: 1) economic regulation regarding tariffs; 2) technical regulation for safety purposes; 3) inspections, coupled with the powers to enforce regulation and issue sanctions, when applicable; and 4) trackage and hauling rights.

During its first two years of existence, the ARTF has focussed its resources on complying with the immediate and time-driven commitments contained in the different legal documents. For example, the creation decree states that the agency needs to issue its organisation manual within 180 days from its publication or the Article 8 of the transitory clauses of the LRSF, which states that ARTF needs to issue a noise emission technical regulation within 60 days after the creation.

Despite the recent reforms to the rail regulatory framework, there is a need to assess the role of the agency to separate regulation and promotion duties. An example of the roles that need to be further clarified is the promotion of the rail network. According to the LRSF, the ARTF has as a function the promotion of the expansion and usage of the rail network. The accomplishment of this function requires the establishment of specific goals in co-ordination with the DGDFM to avoid conflicts with other regulatory duties. The agency faces competing objectives regarding its regulatory role in the rail sector and the promotion and expansion of the system, which in principle should be the sole responsibility of the DGDFM. See Box 1.2 for an OECD country example on the clarity of role of a regulator.

Another issue arises with the lack of installed capacity for ARTF to carry out inspections, which prevents it from discharging its duties properly. Nowadays the SCT centres support the ARTF on inspection activities. However, this co-ordination is not made through formal agreements, which can create tensions in the effectiveness of the inspection process to meet the agency's standards.

Additionally, the regulatory framework for sanctions and fines is yet to be developed through specific guidelines for their application.

Finally, as mentioned before, the agency still faces severe constraints due to lack of personnel. Since the creation of the agency, arrangements were made to transfer staff from the DGFDM to ARTF, yet this process has not been completed.

> **Box 1.2. The role clarity principle in regulator: country example**
>
> **Federal Institute of Telecommunications of Mexico**
>
> The 2013 telecommunications reform in Mexico created the Federal Institute of Telecommunications (IFT), as the agency in charge of sector regulation and antitrust. The Law of Telecommunications and Broadcasting states the faculties of both the IFT and the Ministry of Communications and Transport (former regulator of the market).
>
> The IFT is an autonomous body with legal personality and own assets. It is in charge of regulating, promoting and supervising the use and exploitation of the radio-electrical spectrum, orbital resources, public telecom networks and the concession of broadcasting and telecommunications. It regulates the access to infrastructure and other essential inputs. It is also in charge of the technical guidelines regarding infrastructure and equipment to access the telecom network. Finally, it is the authority on antitrust issues for the telecommunication market.
>
> On the other hand, the tasks of the Ministry of Telecommunications and Transport are oriented towards the promotion of the market. This includes activities such as policy planning to ensure universal coverage, collaborate on international agreements on telecom, acquire infrastructure, and so forth.
>
> From the point of view of the role clarity principle, the complete separation of the regulatory policy and promotion activities in two institutions makes more efficient the implementation of both tasks, as now they do not compete for financial resources, personnel, priorities, amongst others.
>
> According to the strength of the institutional network in each country, the role clarity principle could require a formal separation of powers to grant autonomy in the decision-making. Formerly, the Ministry of Communications and Transport was the institution in charge of the promotion but at the same time, it was the head of the deconcentrated regulatory body. As such, the Ministry approved the budget of the regulatory body, negotiated it with the Ministry of Finance and finally, assigned it to the regulator. Thus, there was a risk that the Ministry may have a potential influence over the performance of the regulator and its policy execution.

9. *Preventing undue influence and maintain trust: the ARTF has yet to improve its regulatory framework and develop formal practices to build-up trust and support decision-making. Recent legal modifications granting de jure technical independence are a relevant step forward, but further institutional arrangements will ensure an effective operation based on trust and reputation.*

The ARTF needs to stay close to the stakeholders as it can learn about the industry, understand the effects of regulatory decision and the potential impact on the public. The ARTF requires also co-ordination with public agencies to deploy an integrated strategy. A basic requirement to keep a strong and effective relation with relevant actors is a planned, institutionalised and public agenda on stakeholder engagement. See Box 1.3 for some country examples.

Independence demands more efforts on transparency and accountability. The ARTF however, does not have a yearly planned agenda to work with stakeholders. The evidence shows that ARTF meets continuously with regulated firms but these are neither formalised nor planned. Additionally, co-ordination with public entities with shared responsibilities is limited, reactive and done on case-by-case basis.

Transparency and accountability are strong tools to ensure trust. The ARTF complies with the legal obligations but there is a need to increase actions on these matters.

> **Box 1.3. Preventing undue influence and maintain trust: some country examples**
>
> **Government's expectations and regulators' responses in Australia**
>
> The Australian Government's Statement of Expectations (SoE) outlines its expectations about the role and responsibilities of the Australian Competition and Consumer Commission (ACCC), as well as its relationship with the Government, issues of transparency and accountability, and operational matters. This is part of the efforts for the good corporate governance of agencies and for reducing regulatory burdens on business and the community. The SoE states that the ACCC must act independently and objectively in the performance of its functions and in the exercise of its powers. The ACCC in turn provides a Statement of Intent (SoI) outlining how it proposes to meet these expectations.
>
> The Australian Energy Regulator has a similar SoE with the Council of Australian Governments Energy Council (COAGEC). This SoE outlines the expectations of compliance with its functions and implements a work programme that supports the objectives set out in the national energy legislation. The SoE sets out its work programme for regulating energy networks and markets, and the benchmarks that will measure its performance; it also sets out how it aims to achieve the principles of accountability and transparency, efficient regulation and effective engagement with stakeholders and other energy markets.
>
> **Regular dialogue with operators and consumers in Italy**
>
> Since 2015, the AEEGSI has a Permanent Observatory of Energy, Water and District Heating Regulation to facilitate a continuous dialogue with representatives of national associations and to report on AEEGSI activities, within a broader developing process aimed at enhancing AEEGSI accountability.
>
> The Observatory's functions are mainly to:
>
> - Increase stakeholders engagements in the decision making processes, with particular regard to market and infrastructure regulation and to consumer protection;
> - Facilitate the acquisition of data and information that may contribute to the preparation of RIA, as well as for the *ex post* evaluation of policies and implemented decisions of the regulator;
> - Promote the preparation of consultation documents on matters within the responsibilities of the regulator;
> - Acquire from representatives of consumer groups, users and end customers, suggestions for evaluating the actual results of the implementation of commitments of regulated entities.
>
> Source: (OECD, 2016[5]), Being an Independent Regulator, The Governance of Regulators. http://dx.doi.org/10.1787/9789264255401-en.

> 10. *Decision making and governing body structure for independent regulators: The head of the ARTF is a single member freely appointed and removed by the President of Mexico – meaning that there is no defined period for the position. The single member model holds more capture risks and lacks of internal checks and balances in the decision-making processes.*

The ARTF's creation decree defined it as a deconcentrated body with technical, operational and managerial capacity.[3] Notwithstanding, the risk of biased decisions is high due to lack of conditions allowing actual independence, for example, the non-existence of fixed appointment periods and removal criteria. In fact, the Minister of Communications and Transport appoints and removes directly the head of the ARTF.

On the other hand, there is no regulation requiring neither a public contest for the appointment of the head of the ARTF nor establishing the necessary technical competences. This situation can lead to undesired political influence and unfitted profiles in the position. See Box 1.4 for country examples of a decision making body of an economic regulator.

> **Box 1.4. Decision-making and government body structure for economic regulators: country examples**
>
> **Mexico's Federal Institute of Telecommunications (IFT)**
>
> The Federal Institute of Telecommunications has a board of seven commissioners, the President and six members. The IFT has to follow a constitutional-defined process for appointing commissioners. First, the candidates must prove their experience and technical training relevant for the sector. The candidates' application is analysed by an Evaluation Committee, which is comprised by the heads of the Central Bank of Mexico, the National Institute for the Evaluation of Education, and the National Institute of Statistics and Geography – autonomous bodies from the government of Mexico.
>
> Thereafter, the Committee conducts a technical exam which is prepared by at least two universities. The Committee propose between 3 and 5 candidates to the President of the Republic. The President nominates one of the candidates to the Senate, and it has to be endorsed by at least two thirds. If the Senate does not approve the candidate, the President has to select another one from the Committee's proposal and repeat the process. The process would be repeated until a candidate is approved or until there is just one candidate left.
>
> According to the Constitution, the appointment of the IFT is for a fixed period of time and the removal of the commissioners is only under specific situations. Thus, the President of Mexico or the Congress cannot remove directly the members of the board.
>
> The appointment process of the ITF and the Competition Commission of Mexico (both modified through the Competition constitutional reform of Mexico) is one of the strongest practices across OECD countries as it holds a based-experience and education public tender.
>
> **France's Commission for Energy Regulation (CRE)**
>
> The French energy code provides that Board of Commissioners of the Commission for Energy Regulation comprises six members, while respecting parity between men and women. The President of the Board is appointed by a decree of the President of the Republic upon proposal of the Prime Minister, following public hearings and a formal opinion on the nominee expressed by the relevant parliamentary committees. Three members of the Board are also appointed by a decree of the President of the Republic, one of them upon proposal of the Minister in charge of the French Overseas Territories based on the person's knowledge and experience of non-interconnected areas. The Presidents of the National Assembly and the Senate appoint two additional members of the Board each (one based on the person's knowledge and qualifications in the field of data protection and the other in the field of local energy services).
>
> **Italy's Regulatory Authority for Electricity, Gas and Water**
>
> The Italian Regulatory Authority for Electricity Gas and Water was established in 1995 by a Law, which defines the Authority's governance system, including Board structure, the appointment mechanism, and members' requisites. The Authority's Board is composed of five commissioners: the President and four members.

All commissioners are appointed by a decree of the President of the Republic following nomination by the Council of Ministers on the basis of a proposal by the Minister of Economic Development. Nominations are submitted to the relevant parliamentary committees for scrutiny, and the appointment is based on a two-thirds majority vote. In 2011, following a spending review which involved all public sector, the number of Board members was reduced from five to three.

The Prime Minister nominates a Chairman, in agreement with the Minister for Communications. The nominee is subject to the binding opinion of the relevant parliamentary committees of the Senate and the Chamber of Deputies, which can hold hearings of the nominee. Following a favourable opinion by two-thirds of the members of each relevant parliamentary committee, the Chairman is appointed by a decree of the President of the Italian Republic. In 2011 the number of Board members was reduced from 9 to 5.

Source: (OECD, 2018[6]), Driving Performance at Ireland's Commission for Regulation of Utilities, The Governance of Regulators. http://dx.doi.org/10.1787/9789264190061-en; Federal Law of Telecommunications and Broadcasting (*Ley Federal de Telecomunicaciones y Radiodifusión*).

> 11. *Accountability and transparency: The ARFT regularly publishes information on safety and other indicators in the rail sector; however, this information is limited in scope. Moreover, the agency is not currently accountable to Congress, nor it has practices to promote accountability to other stakeholders besides the SCT and the SHCP.*

The ARTF publishes quarterly statistical information about cargo, tariffs, locomotives, cars, equipment, lines, etc. in the web portal (www.gob.mx/artf). In addition, since 2016, the agency produces quarterly safety reports, which did not exist before. Safety reports include information regarding accidents, theft and vandalism in the Mexican National Railway System public and transparent. Besides, the ARTF produces a yearly report with its main activities – two new indicators of the report are part of the Strategic Indicators of the INEGI.

Currently, the ARTF is accountable according to the requirements of the applicable laws. This includes obligations to provide information on its website on salaries and other organisational information. It is also accountable to SCT and SHCP, but not to congress. However, the ARTF can increase the level and scope of concepts to be accountable. For example, performance indicators, clear objectives and goals are not yet established. See Box 1.5 for a country example on practices of accountability and transparency.

Box 1.5. Accountability and transparency in the UK Office of Rail and Road (ORR)

Formally, the ORR is accountable solely to the Parliament. While members of the Board are appointed by the Minister they are not accountable to him/her but, as noted above, they are appointed to be independent of Ministerial control. The Minister is unable to direct the regulator or to overrule regulatory decisions. While the Minister may guidance rarely done and always done publicly through a published letter. However while the Secretary of State can provide guidance and make representations, he cannot direct the Board.

Along with the ORR's formal accountability to Parliament, there are several measures in place to ensure that this accountability is tested. Firstly, the ORR publishes an annual business plan which provides its strategic objectives and provides a number of measures, both quantitative and qualitative around those measures. The business plan identifies medium and long-term outcomes under each of its strategic objectives. The plan then notes a number of activities taken from the former work programme that are expected to contribute to achieving the longer term outcomes specified in the plan. This is a strong accountability mechanism that commits the ORR to achieving and reporting on a number of goals that, taken together, provide a good picture of the operational success or otherwise of the regulator.

Along with the business plan, the ORR has a requirement to publish an annual report, which is enforced by the National Audit Office (NAO). The Annual Report summarises the key activities and events of the reporting year against the framework of the objectives set out in the business plan. This is a key tool in terms of both accountability and transparency, as it provides substantial performance information in a format that is easy to understand and assess.

While the ORR has an internal requirement to publish all major decisions, there are also statutory and legal requirements to publish certain types of decisions and give reasons supporting the pronouncements. The ORR must maintain a public register of all decisions relating to licences, access agreements, exemptions, consents and enforcement action in respect of its rail economic functions. On the safety side, it publishes details of all improvement and prohibition enforcement notices served on business and prosecutions.

Moreover, the ORR is required to participate as a witness and answer questions or provide evidence to Parliamentary Committees. These committees, the Transport Select Committees and the Public Accounts Committee scrutinise the ORR's work performance in their roles overseeing government policy and performance.

Source: (OECD, 2016[7]), Governance of Regulators' Practices: Accountability, Transparency and Co-ordination, Paris, http://dx.doi.org/10.1787/9789264255388-en.

> 12. Stakeholder Engagement: The ARTF has no proper communication channels with stakeholders, as there is no planned agenda elaborated in advance. Besides, the current meetings are scattered during the year without public records. The ARTF on the other hand, follows a strong consultation process for draft regulations.

The ARTF conducts frequent meetings with stakeholders such as regulated firms and public entities. Most of the time, the sessions take place when stakeholders request them or when the ARTF reacts to specific circumstances. Besides, the follow-up process lacks of proper records. See Box 1.6 for a country example on stakeholder engagement.

Co-ordination between the ARTF and public entities is scarce and depends on case-by-case. For instance, communication with COFECE is neither recurrent nor based on prevention.

The main contact points between the ARTF and its stakeholders are the programmed meetings and the consultation process during the draft of regulations, which is managed by CONAMER. However, this engagement is limited due to the restrictions ARTF faces to issue regulation due to the one-in one-out rule.

Box 1.6. Stakeholder Engagement: Corporate strategy and annual forward work programme of OFGEM in the United Kingdom

The Office of Gas and Electricity Markets of the United Kingdom has developed a corporate strategy that sets out, amongst other things, Ofgem's mission, outcomes, regulatory approaches, priority activities. Ofgem has also separately published regulatory stances which are principles for drafting policy. These regulatory stances are:

- Promoting effective competition to deliver for consumers.
- Driving value in monopoly activities through competition and incentive regulation.

- Supporting innovation in technologies, systems and business models.
- Managing risk for efficient and sustainable energy.
- Protecting the interests of consumers in vulnerable situations.

Ofgem establishes an annual forward work programme for setting its corporate strategy. It initially publishes a draft forward work programme, and then seeks submissions, which are considered for finalising the forward work programme. For example, Ofgem's draft Forward Work Programme for 2017-18 was released for consultation on December 2016 for a 3 months period for submissions. The final version was published on March 2017.

The draft forward work programme for 2017-18 sets out key initiatives in which were identified specific pieces of work that Ofgem considered that would deliver the greatest benefit to consumers given its resources. The initiatives presented were:

- Enabling a better functioning retail market;
- Facilitating the energy transition;
- Learning from the first RIIO* framework and setting RIIO-2 up for success;
- Introducing competition in monopoly areas;
- Becoming an authoritative source of quality analysis.

The forward work programme also sets out Ofgem's budget for the period, and includes regulatory and e-serve performance indicators and deliverables for each of the pieces of work under the initiatives.

Note: * Revenue= Incentives + Innovation + Outputs.
Source: (OECD, 2018[6]), Driving Performance at Ireland's Commission for Regulation of Utilities, http://dx.doi.org/10.1787/9789264190061-en.

13. Funding: the ARTF has limitations to get the necessary funding it needs to accomplish the objectives and functions stated in the legal framework.

The ARTF analyses its budget internally and subsequently negotiate with SCT the amount of resources for the next fiscal year. The SCT can however, limit the budget as it is the final institution accountable of the sector. After two years of the ARTF's existence, it is important to analyse the actual needs of financial resources and personnel in order to accomplish the objectives of the agency.

The agency is yet to incorporate appropriate staff in sufficient number to carry out the tasks relating to its organisation and attributions. The regulator's staff must be aligned in number and profiles with the regulator's objectives and goals. Furthermore, it is important that the regulator develop the ability to manage human resources autonomously and effectively.

The budget of the ARTF may depend on the SCT's financial resources. A direct source of funding can help to ensure financial independence. For instance, the ARTF can get and fully administrate the resources from fines and the licence fees established in the concessions – the current fee is 2% of annual revenues and goes directly to the SHCP. See Box 1.7 for an example of funding arrangements from the United Kingdom.

Box 1.7. Funding in the UK's Office of Rail and Road

The Office of Rail and Road can work with more autonomy from the central government as its activities are funded by the rail industry and by the Department of Transport. On the rail side, it receives the funding from the rail industry (through license fees and safety levies). From the road activities, it receives a direct grant from the Department of Transport. The economic regulation funding comes from Network Rail's licence fee. It also recovers costs from its work related to other networks not owned by Network Rail. The health and safety activities are funded through a safety levy, which is based on the turnover of each railway service provider.

Table 1.2. Rail's Health and Safety Regulation levy scheme

Company turnover	Railway safety levy
<GBP 1 million	GBP 0
GBP £1 – 5 million	GBP 1 000
GBP 5 10 million	GBP 5 000
Over £10 million	Apportioned according to relevant turnover. As a guide for budgetary purposes, levy payments have in the past been around 0.1% of reported relevant turnover

For the 2018-19 period, the ORR received GBP 30.3m from the rail industry that represented around 93% of its total income:

- 51% corresponding to health and safety regulation
- 42% to economic regulation
- 7% corresponded to the direct funding from the Department of Transport.

Figure 1.1. Total income from ORR's rail and roads functions

2018-19

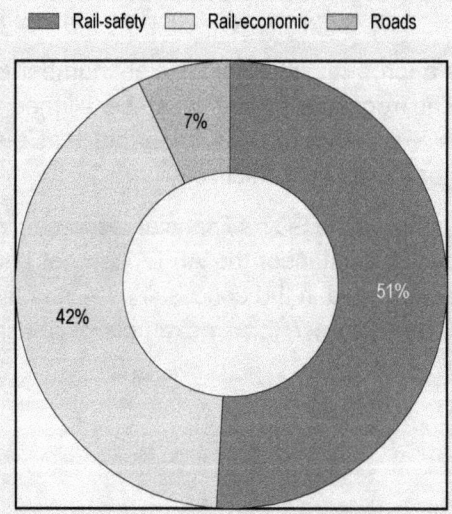

> An element to highlight in this scheme is that, there is no potential for cross-subsidies between these three funding streams.
>
> The majority of its expenditure is on staff costs and the overheads that are necessary for them to carry out their work, such as building maintenance and IT.
>
> By November 2018, the ORR had 316 employees and the staff costs expenditure was of GBP 19.8m (GBP 1.8 m per month approximately); this represents around 65% of the annual budget.
>
> Even when ORR's budget is not decided by the executive branch or approved by the Parliament, to ensure transparency of the budget management, the ORR sends to the Parliament and publishes on its website an annual report with detailed financial indicators.
>
> According to an Oxford's Economics paper on the economic contribution of rail in the United Kingdom published in 2018, the direct and indirect contribution of railway's related activities goes up to GBP 36.4bn in terms of contribution to the GDP, and generates around 600 000 jobs. This represents around 2% of the GDP.
>
> Source: (ORR, 2018[8]), Business Plan 2018-19, UK Government, London. https://orr.gov.uk/__data/assets/pdf_file/0006/27465/orr-business-plan-2018-19.pdf (accessed 2 March 2019); and (Godden, 2018[9]), The Economic Contribution of UK Rail 2018, Oxford Economics, London. https://www.oxfordeconomics.com/recent-releases/06ec32db-6550-44ed-ac64-6502b9530867 (accessed 2 March 2019).

14. Performance evaluation: the ARTF does not have a performance evaluation or indicators (internal and/or external) that help the decision-making in the regulatory process.

Currently, ARTF does not have mechanisms to assess its own performance and the one of the sector. However, the agency aims to implement the National System of Railway Indicators which will publish information of the Mexican railway system for which there is no further information yet. At the time of preparing this report, the ARTF reported that it is preparing 12 indicators, which it plans to put for public consultation.

Indicators that evaluate the performance of the industry can be developed based on the analysis of collected data. This information would ensure that all railway companies have access to relevant indicators, which can contribute to improve compliance and the performance of the whole sector.

For regulators, performance indicators need to fit the purpose of the assessment, which is a systematic, analytical evaluation of the regulator's activities with the objective of seeking reliability and usability of the regulator's activities. The development of these indicators can help identify problem areas, orient decisions, track progress and identify priorities. Organisational and financial performance as well as the existence and effective use of tools are important aspects that should be measured.

> **Box 1.8. Italian Regulatory Authority for Electricity, Gas and Water performance indicators & assessment framework**
>
> The Italian Regulatory Authority for Electricity, Gas and Water (AEEGSI) tracks both service quality (outcomes) and the efficiency and effectiveness of the regulatory process (inputs and outputs). The aim is to improve the regulator's performance and the quality of the services provided to consumers.
>
> **Outcomes**
>
> The AEEGSI defines outcome indicators to design incentive-based regulation and monitor the evolution of the regulated sectors. For instance, AEEGSI has been able to progressively increase the quality of

supply through incentives and penalties paid to and by distributors by measuring the average duration of interruptions of electricity supply.

The AEEGSI conducts an annual review to monitor the evolution of the energy retail markets and eventually adjust regulatory provisions to foster competition and enhance consumer protection. The annual review uses, for instance, the HHI index (Herfindahl-Hirschman Index) to measure:

- competition
- the ratio between complaints and served customers to capture the quality of the interaction with energy suppliers
- the share of consumers changing their supplier (i.e. switching rate) to track the sector's maturity (consumers' awareness and trust, suppliers' proactivity and the regulatory environment).

By assigning a standard cost for unit of energy not supplied, it is also possible to evaluate the direct impact on the final users through a cost-benefit analysis on the consumer side, considering incentives paid to distributors and avoided interruptions.

Inputs and outputs

The AEEGSI links the Strategic and Operational planning process to its objectives, which are assessed in terms of inputs and outputs. For each objective, inputs are mainly determined by the costs of the employed workforce. On an annual basis, each Department defines the working hours and the relative annual costs an objective has required to be met.

During the regulatory process, each deliverable may be considered an output to be associated to an objective. In order to distinguish contributions from different units, production processes have been broken down and intermediate outputs are also considered, as long as they could be identified as final products of specific phases of a process or sub-processes.

Considering the peculiarity of the regulation and the rapidly evolving regulated sectors, a quantitative estimation of output has been centred on the complexity inherent to their realisation. This feature is analysed summing indicators to be assigned in a dedicated IT information system, related to four parameters:

- Problem solving: it is measured with reference to the necessary professional skills, the discretion applied to solving the case, as well as the ordinary or innovative feature of the case in question.
- Effort: the intensity of the commitment sustained to bring the output to fruition, such as the quantitative dimension of the activities to be carried out, the severity of the approached internal procedure, and the intensity of the interactions with other stakeholders.
- Co-ordination among units: the need to make use of contribution of other organisational units and from which it is possible to infer a customer-supplier relationship.
- Time compression: the need to achieve output in a shorter time due to exogenous and unforeseen or foreseeable causes, such as the need to modify the current planning of activities.
- Performance assessment is carried out analysing, for each objective, the evolution of input and output indicators through the regulatory period considered in the Strategic and Operational Plans and their correlations to evaluate the overall efficiency and identify potential improvements.

Source: (OECD, 2018[6]), Driving Performance at Ireland's Commission for Regulation of Utilities, Paris, http://dx.doi.org/10.1787/9789264190061-en.

Recommendations related to rail regulation

- ARTF's should evaluate if and where introduction of additional trackage rights of the kinds provided for in the concession agreements could unlock significant gains in network-wide efficiency and competitiveness for Mexican industry without undermining the sustainability of the rail services provided already by the concessions. A good network model would be extremely useful in making these assessments and evaluations.
- ARTF should also look into reporting requirements in regard to the location of wagons, as poor service in the return of wagons owned by third parties can readily be used as a non-tariff barrier to competition. Railinc already tracks wagons in international service and extension to domestic traffic might not therefore be too challenging. ARTF should also review existing arrangements for charges for the movement of empty wagons. Both concession holders and third parties see shortcomings in the current situation.
- ARTF's first priority in developing capacity to make the provisions for connectivity and competition in the law fully operational is to establish the basis for tariff regulation, when needed, for both captive shippers and cases of failure to reach agreement on mandated trackage and haulage rights. Such charges will need to cover marginal costs, as stipulated in the Law. For captive shippers, a guideline for identifying abusive prices will need to be established.

  Methodology followed by the US STB might be followed, but its approach has been criticised as being overly complex and expensive to use as well as not resting on solid economic grounds (Pittman, 2010[10]), (TRB, 2015[11]). Alternatives have been proposed in the United States – including econometric analysis of comparable shipments in more competitive conditions, commodity-specific ceilings on mark-ups over variable cost, and location-specific *rate-of-return regulation* – but these have their own drawbacks and have not yet been used in practice.

- ARTF will need to develop a methodology of its own to define maximum tariffs, allowing for a reasonable contribution to the fixed costs of the railway informed by Ramsey-Boiteux pricing theory. The methodology adopted should also aim as far as possible to minimise modelling demands and the need for expensive consultancy to establish whether the thresholds set are met. There are no methods to provide theoretically perfect thresholds for *"abusive"* pricing or *"fair"* regulated tariffs – these are political and philosophical rather than scientific and economic concepts. The expertise of the ARTF should be relied on to set workable values following consultation with both shippers and concession holders. Consultation needs to go beyond a request for opinions on draft rules and involve thorough, but not protracted, discussion. An operational procedure is urgently needed, and in this as in so many contexts, the best may be the enemy of the good.
- ARTF should also examine the availability of interline services and develop procedures for setting regulated tariffs where concessions fail to offer services. It may be sufficient to interpret a failure to offer a tariff for an interline service as equivalent to setting an abusive tariff. Shippers are naturally hesitant to make complaints against railways on which they depend for transport services, in Mexico and elsewhere in North America, so the ARTF will need to take initiatives to monitor operation of the market.

  It should be kept in mind that overall the performance of the concessions and the system established in 1995 has been exceptional. The object of intervention by ARTF is not to overturn the system but to identify the areas of opportunity that certainly exist for developing rail markets. Interline services may present more opportunity for gains in the short term than additional trackage rights, with minimal damage to the existing markets of concession holders.

- SCT and the government more broadly needs to begin work on its vision for the railway system post 2027 without delay, as the investment cycle of railways is much longer than 9 years. ARTF's expert opinion should be sought in this regard.

An efficient system should continue to be organised around exclusive concessions but parts of the market might be suitable for more use of broad trackage rights. As in the United States, the eventual system will have to be based on a sustainable balance between exclusivity and intramodal as well as intermodal competition. The model of fully commercial railways is the most effective and financially sustainable option for essentially freight railways like those of North America. The framework established in Mexico has proved successful and durable, and a policy of incremental improvement rather than radical change is more suitable.

See Box 1.9 for the Activities carried out to enhance the performance of the railway system by the ARTF 2018-2024 administration.

Box 1.9. Activities carried out to enhance the performance of the railway system by the ARTF 2018-2024 administration

Restructuring of Federal Rail Licenses (LFF)

Taking into consideration the public passenger transport projects that are currently being developed in the country, ARTF should pay special attention to the technical, operational and regulatory regulation in public freight rail transport and passengers.

In order to improve the safety in the operation of the provision of public services of freight, passenger and / or mixed transport, the Agency is evaluating the restructuring of the categories that currently exist for the issuance of LFFs, taking into account the delimitation between the functions performed by the personnel involved in the rail freight and passenger operation, as well as the personnel involved in the maintenance and conservation of the general communication routes, considering that these activities could intervene in the operation of the services provided therein.

Derived from the above, the Agency has sought the exchange of information with companies dedicated to training, such is the case of the *Centro de Formacion Ferroviaria Adofer, S.A. de CV*, which conducted a study of the "Railway Licenses in Mexico, Europe and America", which aims to publicise an overview of the granting of the various existing rail licenses in Mexico, Europe and America, identify the requirements necessary for issuance, applicable regulations and make a comparison of them. Likewise, identify those licenses that are not found in the Mexican rail system and that can be used according to the nature of the functions of the existing posts in the country.

The ARTF, in order to carry out the restructuring of the LFFs, should take into account the technological developments, studies and cutting-edge research worldwide related to rail freight and passenger transport, which could be implemented, for the update of the categories of the LFF.

Likewise, ARTF intends to carry out working groups with the concessionaires and assignees of the National Rail System to assess and agree on the updating of the existing categories of the LFF, taking into consideration the personnel involved in the operation of the railway equipment and the one that takes part in the maintenance activities, with the aim of improving the safety in the railway operation.

Collaboration agreement between the ARTF and National Autonomous University of Mexico (UNAM)

It will allow the Agency, through UNAM, to carry out road engineering studies, considering the danger index of railroad crossings, to assess the current impact they have on vehicular traffic and propose solutions to improve mobility and safety in the said crosses; studies that will provide the Agency with a planning and decision-making tool, which allow identifying the actions to be carried out in each of the crossings that are studied in urban areas and population centers, applying the current regulations such as the technical regulations NOM-050-SCT2-2017, "Provision for the signaling of crossings at the level of roads and streets with railways" and NOM-034-SCT2-2011, "Horizontal and vertical signaling of urban roads and highways".

In this context, the integration of security committees in the federal states of Mexico with the highest incidence is promoted: Coahuila, Durango, State of Mexico, Michoacán, Nuevo León, Veracruz, in order to monitor the operation of the crossings that are identified as susceptible if financed by the National Safety Fund for Railroad Crossings.

Likewise, the survey and georeferenced registration of the existing crossings in the Mexican Rail System that will allow to know the universe to be considered for future fund financing is carried out.

Source: ARTF 2018-2024 administration.

- The Agency should establish a system of forward planning in which all the needs to issue or update regulatory instruments are identified, in a horizon of six months to one year, as it is now indicated in the new General Law of Regulatory Improvement. This planning should include both technical regulation, and all the other legal instruments, for instance, by-laws (*reglamentos*), manuals, and guidelines. This planning may effectively identify the efforts ahead and may help determine the resources needed to maintain the regulatory framework updated, including the need of regulation to be eliminated to comply with the one-in, one-out rule.
- One way to comply with the one-in, one-out rule is to take advantage of deadwood regulation of the SCT to compensate the regulatory costs that potential regulation of the ARTF may create. Thus, in the current situation, it is important to develop a joint SCT-ARTF strategic plan for the emission of regulation. The participation of the parties might facilitate the co-ordination efforts for the introduction of new regulations by the ARTF.
- Additionally, the ARTF and the SCT may seek to reach an agreement with the CONAMER to seek a moratorium or an exception to the one-in, one-out rule to issue the most pressing regulation or the one with the most significant impact for the performance of the rail sector.
- The SCT, SHCP, SFP and the agency should co-ordinate to complete without further delay the transfer of staff to the agency according to the original plans.

  Besides the transfer of the pending officials, it is important to conduct an analysis about the minimum human resources and technical profiles that the ARTF needs to perform its duties.

  Along with the staff agreed to be relocated, it is also necessary to finish the transfer of information from the DGDFM to the ARTF so the agency can perform according to objectives.
- ARTF and the SCT should work together to agree and prepare the necessary reforms to the legal framework to include ARTF in the process of assessing and granting of concessions. The ARTF could provide nonbinding technical opinions on regulatory matters. Besides strengthening the technical and regulatory aspects of the concession, this arrangement may help to deepen the co-ordination between the agency and the ARTF after the concession in granted, in favor of a better regulatory performance of both parties.

Recommendations on governance

- The regulatory framework that defines the role and functions of ARTF should be reviewed to strive for a reform that focus the Agency´s functions on regulatory roles, while allocating the promotion duties to DGDFM. In the short term, the ARTF should create a strategy document to define its priorities between its current regulatory and promotion duties.

- An assessment of the inspection duties of the ARTF should be carried out in order to define the resource needs to discharge this function properly. A short and long-term strategy to comply with these duties should be defined, considering formal co-operation agreements with the SCT centres while ARTF acquires its own capacities. See Box 1.10 for a short description of the activities carried out by the 2018-2024 administration of ARTF to enhance the performance of the inspections duties of the Agency.

> **Box 1.10. Activities carried out to enhance the performance of the inspections by the ARTF 2018-2024 administration**
>
> - **Updating of specific ARTF areas through training**: the model includes continuous improvement of inspections and supervisions focusing on four elements: infrastructure, operation, equipment and auxiliary services
> - **Harmonisation of criteria in the undertaking of inspections**: harmonisation of the terms of inspection requisition in the three zones of Mexico (north, centre, south); Notification to the ARTF of the type of information requested by the Rail Transport Departments to the concessionaires / assignees
> - **Programme of smart verification**. the objectives are:
>   - Make intelligent use of the assigned financial ceiling, optimising the resources granted;
>   - Schedule and execute verifications focused on quality and not quantity;
>   - Contribute to the concessionaire's safety tasks to make rail transport more efficient; and
>   - Increase the technical capacity of the inspectors through ongoing training
>
>   The programme comprises four stages: planning, execution, evaluation, and follow up
> - **Integral programme of inspections for 2019**: in includes in the short term the inspection of the complete system of the concession rail network, and in the short to medium term the inspections of the auxiliary rail lines without use. The programme will be carried out through Intensive verification operations, in which personnel from both the ARTF and the SCT centres will participate. The intensive verification operations will follow the following key criteria:
>   - Railway Security;
>   - Strategic corridors for the development of the Mexico;
>   - Accident rate;
>   - High risk corridors (for instance, hydrocarbon); and
>   - Potentially important rail lines without use.
> - **Development of the automated system Rail Verification Module Project**:, it will allow automated institutional system to incorporate the information generated in the railway inspection processes into a technology platform, reducing the criteria of human perception in order to standardise the consistency of the data, time reduction, shielding of the information generated and obtained, thereby reinforcing the safety and competitiveness of this mode of transport.
>
> Source: ARTF 2018-2024 administration.

- Issue the necessary guidelines and other regulatory instruments to put in effect an effective sanctioning system.
- The ARTF should consider adopting guidelines as part of its regulatory framework and establish a strategy to avoid subjectivity in decisions and reduce the risk of regulatory capture, which can arise from government agencies, regulated entities and the public.

    This might include the establishment of formal channels of communications, as they may provide relevant information about the quality of the rail service. A clear and transparent engagement method and its monitoring create trust in the regulator. This engagement process can involve other institutions as COFECE and CONAMER.

    The build-up of trust can be strengthened with formal and public processes to co-ordinate with other public agencies with shared responsibilities. For example, with COFECE the Law on the Regulation of Rail Services mandates co-ordination when there is suspicion of lack of competition. Thus, both institutions should establish a detailed process indicating timing and resolutions of the intervention request.

- It is important that the ARTF establishes a yearly planned and public agenda with dates and topics to cover with the stakeholders. As it will be seen in the stakeholder engagement principle, this agenda should involve the participation of the relevant actors in the designing of public policies. The establishment of the agenda should be aligned with the regulatory objectives of the ARTF.
- The Agency should consider establishing practices on accountability and transparency that go beyond its current obligations that derive from the national framework. For instance, the ARTF should improve the quantity and the quality of information it publishes in its web portal in handily formats.
- The SCT and the Agency should consider exploring alternative models for the governing body of the ARTF. In this process, the SCT and the Agency should weigh in the advantages of having a governing body with arms-length distance of political cycles and decisions, which can help the agency discharge its regulatory duties more effectively.
- In order to strengthen accountability and transparency practices, the ARTF should boost its reporting mechanisms by considering submitting yearly reports to Congress as a separate item from the reporting of the SCT. Proactive mechanism could also be adopted to submit the report to other key stakeholders and seek their feedback, such as industry association and sector experts.

    For this purpose, the agency should assess the type of information it requires to comply with its objectives, in order to offer useful and relevant statistical information to its stakeholders. This can be done through an international benchmark and focus groups with relevant actors. In line with the former, another source of accountability and transparency is the evaluation of performance indicators, which is addressed below.

- ARTF has ample opportunities to enhance its practices on stakeholder engagement. This might include establishing yearly plans that set out regular meetings with stakeholders, provisions to record meetings, mechanisms to follow up on issues put forth, and the creation of permanent communication channels.

    Special emphasis should be considered to establish formal communication and engagement activities with entities such as COFECE and CONAMER, in order to maintain a fluid dialogue. This might help ARTF to discharge its regulatory duties more effectively.

    See Box 1.11 for a description of the Activities carried out to boost the stakeholder engagement activities by the ARTF 2018-2024 administration.

> **Box 1.11. Activities carried out to boost the stakeholder engagement practices by the ARTF 2018-2024 administration**
>
> **Rounds of Dialogue to identify improvements to the railway system between users, concessionaire and the ARTF during 2019**
>
> The opportunity areas to improve the Mexican rail system were identified by dividing it into three parts:
>
> - From the user to the concessionaire and Agency;
> - From the concessionaire to the user and the Agency; and
> - From the Agency for the user and the concessionaire.
>
> There have been two meetings with each group, with the following progress:
>
> - ARTF will work with an intermediary and an agreement document will be generated:
>   - Traffic analysis where there is an interline rate to allow continuity, and
>   - The cases of trackage rights that are not being used or where its use is is detrimental to the load.
> - The conversion of cargo from truck to rail will be identified and promoted:
>   - A joint strategy will be made with dealers and user associations,
>   - A policy for intermodal traffic will be sought, and
>   - The no charging of maximum rate in empty cars will be promoted.
> - Users will report the problem of insecurity to add them to the collaboration with the national guard.
>
> As a results of the round of dialogue, the ARTF will:
>
> - Publish on its web portal
>   - Good international practices.
>   - Rights and obligations of users, concessionaires and ARTF, and
>   - Railway projects that affect the efficiency of the sector, for example mobility, level crossings, spurs in disuse, studies to increase railway capacity.
> - Annual training program for the sector
> - Incentives with the Tax Authority for users who invest in rail infrastructure
> - Official conciliation procedure and its documentation, in accordance with Article 112 of the Rail Service Regulation
>
> Source: ARTF 2018-2024 administration.

- In terms of consultation in the drafting of regulation, the ARTF should consider undertaking practices of early consultation more systematically. This entails engaging with stakeholders at the outset of the identification of a problem, before a solution has been clearly identified, and before a draft legal instrument has been prepared.
- The SCT, SHCP and ARTF should review the funding requirements of the agency in order to define the budget the agency needs to discharge its duties effectively.

    In this revision, consideration should be given to implement the necessary reforms to allow ARTF to propose its budget autonomously and negotiate it directly with SHCP, and to exercise this budget independently.

Additionally, these reforms should consider including provisions to give a portion of the fee currently charged to the regulated entities directly to ARTF.

- The ARTF should develop a system of indicators in line with its main functions, which allows the evaluation of its public policy objectives in different periods. Some indicators should be of longer-term nature and focus on the potential impact of the regulatory policy (e.g. number of accidents/distance; freight tariff stability, etc.); however, it is important to mention that these are multidimensional indicators and its evolution is not fully under the control of the ARTF. These targets should be used as a basis for the design and evaluation of the public policy.

   The indicators should include other kinds of metrics such as administrative or managerial indicators, including number of inspections, budget allocation, number of fines imposed, etc. Although these parameters are relevant, it is important to bear in mind that they do not reflect the effectiveness or success of the public policy.

Notes

[1] See Table 3.4. for the list of mandatory trackage and haulage rights included in the concession titles in Mexico.

[2] The most significant of these stalled mandatory trackage rights were for Kansas City Southern Mexico (KCSM) to use track of the Mexican Railways company (*Ferrocarriles mexicanos*, Ferromex). Negotiations over implementation of these rights were protracted for several years, and were unresolved until the acquisition of Ferrosur by Grupo Mexico, owner of Ferromex.

[3] A deconcentrated body in Mexican law is usually an agency at arms-length distance of a ministry, with varying degrees of autonomy.

References

COFECE (2016), *Reporte Preliminar sobre Competencia Efectiva en el Sistema Ferroviario Mexicano [Preliminar report on the Effective Competition in the Mexican Railway System]*.	[1]
COFEMER (2017), *Informe Anual de Desempeño-COFEMER 2016-2017*, http://www.cofemer.gob.mx/docs-bin/dg/Informe_anual_2017.pdf (accessed on 31 January 2018).	[2]
Godden, D. (2018), *The Economic Impact of UK Rail 2018*, Oxford Economics, London, https://www.oxfordeconomics.com/recent-releases/06ec32db-6550-44ed-ac64-6502b9530867.	[9]
OECD (2018), *Driving Performance at Ireland's Commission for Regulation of Utilities*, The Governance of Regulators, OECD Publishing, Paris, https://dx.doi.org/10.1787/9789264190061-en.	[6]
OECD (2016), *Being an Independent Regulator*, The Governance of Regulators, OECD Publishing, Paris, https://dx.doi.org/10.1787/9789264255401-en.	[5]

OECD (2016), *Governance of Regulators' Practices: Accountability, Transparency and Co-ordination*, The Governance of Regulators, OECD Publishing, Paris, https://dx.doi.org/10.1787/9789264255388-en. [7]

OECD (2014), *The Governance of Regulators*, OECD Publishing, Paris, http://dx.doi.org/10.1787/9789264209015-en. [4]

ORR (2018), *Business Plan 2018-19*, ORR, London, https://orr.gov.uk/__data/assets/pdf_file/0006/27465/orr-business-plan-2018-19.pdf (accessed on 3 March 2019). [8]

Pittman, R. (2010), "Against the Stand-Alone-Cost Test in U.S. Freight Rail Regulation", *Journal of Regulatory Economics*, Vol. 38/3, pp. 313-326, https://link.springer.com/content/pdf/10.1007%2Fs11149-010-9130-3.pdf (accessed on 2 March 2019). [10]

TRB (2015), *Modernizing Freight Rail Regulation*, TRB Publications, http://www.trb.org/Publications/Blurbs/172736.aspx. [11]

Trnka, D. and Y. Thuerer (2019), "One-In, X-Out: Regulatory offsetting in selected OECD countries", *OECD Regulatory Policy Working Papers*, No. 11, OECD Publishing, Paris, https://dx.doi.org/10.1787/67d71764-en. [3]

2 Performance of the rail sector of Mexico

This section briefly describes the general performance of the rail sector in Mexico. It comprises an industry assessment, a spatial analysis and an international comparison. The industry review focuses on the economic performance, the product analysis and the market share assessment of the rail sector. The spatial analysis aims at identifying the main rail commercial corridors in the country, as well as their dynamics. Finally, the international analysis provides a general overview of the rail sector within the international arena.

Industry analysis

This section aims to outline a general profile of the rail freight transportation in Mexico since the restructuring of the industry, based on its economic performance. In general, the restructuring of the rail freight industry was successful, as it turned the decreasing tendency on economic performance exhibited during the state control. The economic activity of the rail sector recovered its dynamism. It increased slightly but steadily both its share of freight transported and the tonnage of freight transported. Moreover, the restructuring brought investment again and improved the freight service in comparison with the previous years.

Compared to other modes of transportation, the competitive advantage of the rail transportation is more evident for long hauls. At the same time, rails are usually dependent on connectivity with other modes of transportation to deliver products. For this reason, economic performance is dependent on the degree of connectivity of the rail network, the productivity in logistics and the quality of the infrastructure; but also on the competition playing field that rail firms or corridors (origin – destination segments) face with another railway firms or transportation competitors from other modes. In what follows, the economic profile of the industry is presented.

Economic performance

In 2017, the total tonnage transported in Mexico accounted for 982 million. The freight transported by road was the most important mode with 546.6 tonnes, which represented 55.7% of the sector. The second most important was maritime with 307.6 millions of tonnes, about 31.3%. Rail transportation in contrast, moved 126.6 million of tonnes during 2017 (about 12.9% of the total) and the remaining 0.7 million were moved by air (0.1% of the total).

Railways in Mexico also transport passengers in a unique line for mid distances. In 2017, 56 million people used the *Sub-urban Train*, which represented 1.5% of the total in the country – approximately 1.475 million of passengers *per* kilometre (see Table 2.1).

Table 2.1. Freight and passenger by transportation mode

Millions in 2017

Mode of transport	Tonnes	%	Passengers	%
Road	546.6	55.7	3 701	95.8
Rail	126.6	12.9	56	1.5
Water	307.6	31.3	17	0.4
Air	0.7	0.1	90	2.3
Total	**982**	**100**	**3 864**	**100**

Source: SCT (2018[1]), *Estadística Básica 2017* [Basic Statistics 2017], http://www.sct.gob.mx/transporte-y-medicina-preventiva/autotransporte-federal/estadistica/2017/ (accessed 5 March 2019).

The evolution of the tonnage moved by the type of transport is presented in Figure 2.1 and Table 2.2. As it can be observed, the four modes experienced an increasing tendency. In principle, the gross tonnage increased 62.0% from 606 million tonnes to 982 million for the period 1995-2017. The air transport presented the highest increase of the period with 193.7%, although this mode has the lowest share in terms on tonnage. The rail transport raised 141.2% from 52 million tonnes to 127 million, followed by maritime transportation with an increase of 65.2% from 186 million tonnes to 308 million.

Regarding the share in terms of tonnage, road transportation has had the biggest proportion. In 2017, the road share was 55.7%, a slightly decrease with respect to 1995 with 60.6% (see Table 2.2). Rail transportation in comparison had a 12.9% share in 2017, which gained a steadily increase since 1995 with

8.7%. The maritime share of tonnage rose from 30.7% in 1995 to 31.3% in 2017. Finally, the air transportation showed a share of 0.1% in 2017 from 0.05% in 1995. In general, the information of Table 2.2 shows that the train freight transportation gained share, measured by the tonnage reported between 1995 and 2017. Besides, the data seems to suggest that rail gained share at the expense of road transportation.

Figure 2.1. Evolution of the freight transport

Million tonnes 1995-2017

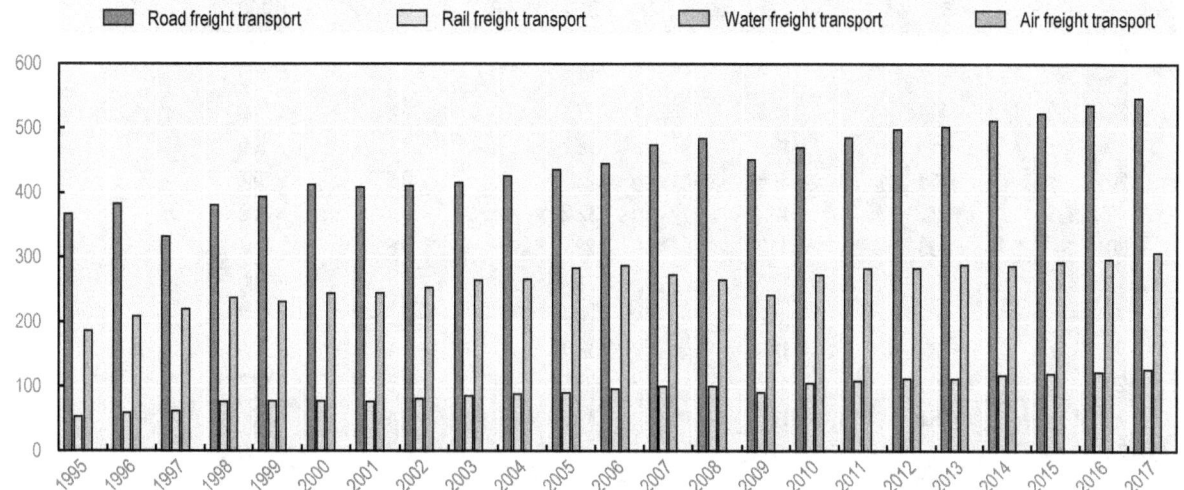

Source: SCT (2018[1]), *Estadística Básica 2017* [Basic Statistics 2017], DOF, CDMX, http://www.sct.gob.mx/transporte-y-medicina-preventiva/autotransporte-federal/estadistica/2017/ (accessed 5 March 2019).

Table 2.2. Freight transportation by year and mode

Million tonnes and percentage

Years	Road	Rail	Maritime	Air	Total
1995	367	52	186	0.3	606
%	60.6	8.7	30.7	0.0	100
1996	383	59	209	0.3	651
%	58.9	9.0	32.1	0.0	100
1997	332	62	220	0.3	614
%	54.1	10.0	35.8	0.1	100
1998	381	76	237	0.4	695
%	54.8	10.9	34.2	0.1	100
1999	394	77	231	0.4	703
%	56.1	11.0	32.9	0.1	100
2000	413	77	244	0.4	735
%	56.2	10.5	33.2	0.1	100
2001	409	76	244	0.4	730
%	56.0	10.4	33.5	0.0	100
2002	411	80	253	0.4	745
%	55.2	10.8	34.0	0.1	100
2003	416	85	265	0.4	766
%	54.3	11.1	34.5	0.1	100
2004	426	88	266	0.5	781

Years	Road	Rail	Maritime	Air	Total
%	54.6	11.3	34.1	0.1	100
2005	436	90	284	0.5	810
%	53.8	11.1	35.0	0.1	100
2006	445	96	287	0.5	829
%	53.7	11.5	34.7	0.1	100
2007	474	100	273	0.6	847
%	55.9	11.8	32.2	0.1	100
2008	484	100	265	0.5	849
%	57.0	11.7	31.2	0.1	100
2009	451	90	242	0.5	784
%	57.5	11.5	30.9	0.1	100
2010	470	105	273	0.6	848
%	55.4	12.3	32.2	0.1	100
2011	486	108	283	0.6	877
%	55.3	12.4	32.2	0.1	100
2012	498	112	283	0.6	894
%	55.7	12.5	31.7	0.1	100
2013	502	112	289	0.6	903
%	55.6	12.4	32.0	0.1	100
2014	511	117	287	0.6	916
%	55.8	12.8	31.3	0.1	100
2015	523	120	293	0.7	936
%	55.9	12.8	31.3	0.1	100
2016	536	122	297	0.7	955
%	56.1	12.8	31.1	0.1	100
2017	547	127	308	0.7	982
%	55.7	12.9	31.3	0.1	100

Source: SCT (2018[1]), Estadística Básica 2017 [Basic Statistics 2017], DOF, CDMX, http://www.sct.gob.mx/transporte-y-medicina-preventiva/autotransporte-federal/estadistica/2017/ (accessed 5 March 2019).

In financial terms, roads in Mexico contributed to 88.3% of the transport value added, measured in Mexican pesos, between 1994 and 2017, followed by air transport with 5.1%, rail with 3.7% and maritime with 2.9% – see Table 2.3. The dominance of the road transport services for cargo is well known. The industry dynamics however, has modified slightly in recent years, as the participation of the rail services has increased. A key point for this result has been the growth in turnover since the restructuring of the state owned monopoly railway.

Table 2.3. Freight transport by mode

As % of the transport GDP

Year	Air	Rail	Water	Road
1995	6.0%	3.0%	4.3%	86.8%
1996	6.7%	3.6%	4.0%	85.7%
1997	5.4%	3.4%	3.2%	88.0%
1998	5.2%	3.5%	2.9%	88.4%
1999	5.3%	2.9%	3.1%	88.8%
2000	5.1%	3.4%	2.9%	88.6%
2001	5.6%	2.9%	3.0%	88.5%
2002	5.5%	3.1%	3.1%	88.3%

Year	Air	Rail	Water	Road
2003	5.0%	3.4%	3.4%	88.2%
2004	4.6%	4.5%	3.8%	87.0%
2005	4.8%	4.6%	3.2%	87.3%
2006	5.5%	4.6%	3.0%	87.0%
2007	5.4%	4.3%	3.1%	87.2%
2008	4.9%	4.1%	3.0%	88.1%
2009	5.3%	4.0%	2.6%	88.0%
2010	5.2%	3.8%	2.6%	88.3%
2011	5.3%	4.1%	2.8%	87.8%
2012	4.6%	4.1%	2.8%	88.6%
2013	4.3%	3.9%	2.7%	89.1%
2014	4.3%	3.6%	2.5%	89.6%
2015	4.5%	3.5%	2.5%	89.5%
2016	4.6%	3.4%	2.4%	89.6%
2017	4.8%	3.4%	2.1%	89.7%
Periods' average	5.1%	3.3%	2.0%	89.5%

Source: INEGI (n.d.[2]), *PIB y cuentas nacionales*, https://www.inegi.org.mx/temas/pib/ (accessed 1 June 2019).

The rail sector in Mexico experienced significant changes since the restructuring of the industry in 1994. Private capitals boosted the railways by improving the quality of the freight services and increased the investments over infrastructure and the participation in the economic activity within the sector – see Figure 2.2 for the evolution of investments in rail lines.

Figure 2.2. Investment by main rail concessionaires in Mexico

Billion MXN

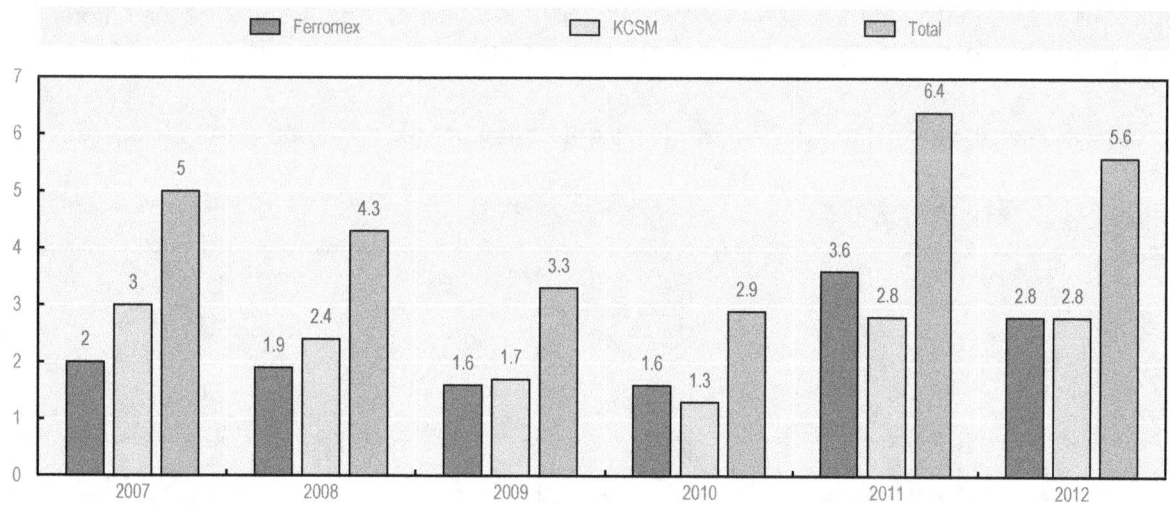

Source: Gobierno de México (2019[3]), Instituto Mexicano del Transporte (Mexican Transport Institute), Queretaro, https://www.gob.mx/imt (accessed 5 March 2019).

Figure 2.3 presents the average growth in gross domestic product (GDP) of the rail transport in percentage for the period 1994-2017. The growth of the railways was the highest of the transport sector with 4.1%; it was 0.1% larger than roads, which is the most important transportation mode in Mexico.

Figure 2.3. Average growth in gross domestic product (GDP) of the freight transport in Mexico between 1994 and 2017

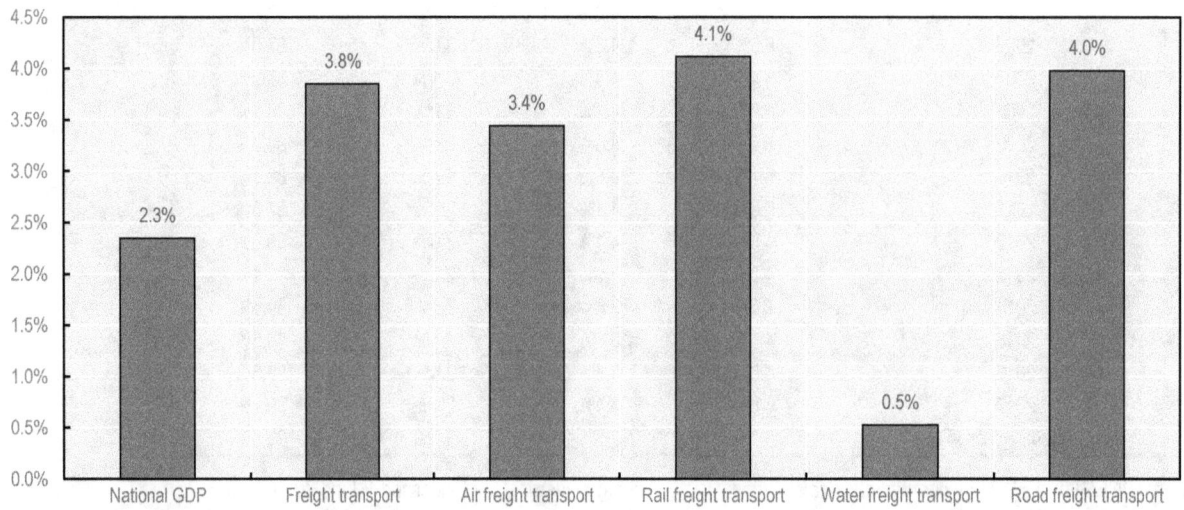

Source: Elaborated with data from INEGI (2019[4]), *Banco de Información Económica* (BIE) (Economic Information Bank), https://www.inegi.org.mx/sistemas/bie/ (accessed 5 March 2019).

Figure 2.4 shows GDP growth of the transport sector on a yearly basis for the period 1994-2017. In general, the data shows there is no clear path in the performance of the rail system. Between 1994 and 2003, the rail sector exhibited periods of sharp growth in economic activity, combined with falls. In this period, in the years of positive growth, the rail transportation mode outperformed transport services as a whole. In contrast, from 2004 to 2017, the year-to-year growth of the railways performed below the national freight industry, with the exception of 2009 and 2010. Overall, it seems that the high rates of growth in the GDP of the rail industry in the immediate years following the 1994 restructuring account for the difference in performance between the freight transport as a whole, and the rail sector between the period 1994-2017.

Figure 2.4. Year to year growth in GDP of the freight transport in Mexico between 1994 and 2017

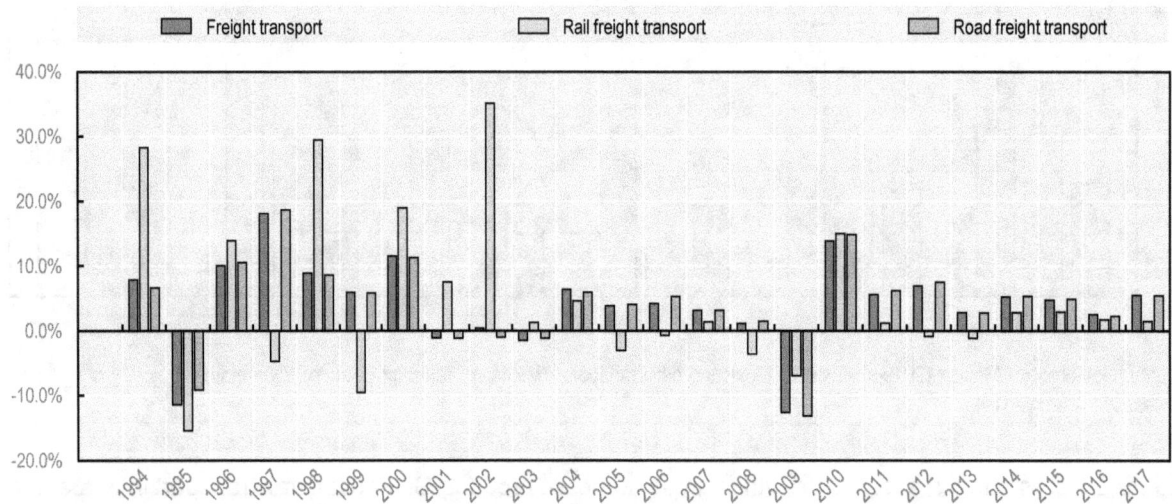

Source: Elaborated with data from INEGI (2019[4]), *Banco de Información Económica (BIE)* (Economic Information Bank), https://www.inegi.org.mx/sistemas/bie/ (accessed 5 March 2019).

The volume of freight transported by railways increased steadily from 2007 to 2017, see Figure 2.5 and Table 2.4. Figure 2.5 shows the behaviour of the freight moved by rail between 2007 and 2017. In general terms it shows there has been an overall increasing tendency, although with periods of falls in 2007-09 and 2011-13.

Table 2.4 shows that in absolute terms, cargo grew from 99.8 million of tonnes in 2007 to 126.9 million in 2017 – an increase of 27.2%, which implied a 2.4% in average per year. Also, the tonne-kilometres carried passed from 77 169 million to 86 332 – an increase of 9 163 million, equivalent to a growth of 11.9% – for the whole period, which represented about 1.1% in yearly basis.

Table 2.4. Rail freight transportation in Mexico

	2007	2008	2009	2010	2011	2012	2013	2014	2015	2016	2017
Tonnes (million)	99.8	99.7	90.3	104.6	108.4	111.6	111.9	116.9	119.6	122.0	126.9
Tonne-km (million)	77 169	74 582	69 185	78 770	79 728	79 353	77 717	80 683	83 401	84 694	86 332

Source: Elaborated by the OECD with data from ARTF (2018[5]), *Anuario Estadístico Ferroviario 2017* (Railway Statistical Yearbook 2017), https://www.gob.mx/artf/acciones-y-programas/anuario-estadistico-ferroviario-2017-152797 (accessed 31 January 2018).

Regarding the cost of freight services, Figure 2.6 presents the evolution of averaged tariffs from 1960 to 2010 for Mexican, Canadian and US lines. The period comprises the breakpoints of the US deregulation, the Canadian privatisation and the granting of private concessions in Mexico. For the Mexican case, there is a gap in statistical information from 1987 to 1998; thus, there are no records of tariffs for such period.

Before the concessions in Mexico, the tariffs paid by customers labelled as *Nacionales de Mexico* (NdeM) (freight only) were lower than the average in the US and Canada. While the Mexican state-national railway firm was in charge of the operation of the freight services, the federal government had to grant a subsidy to cover the negative balance of the firm. For instance, the real tariffs composed by the payment of customers and the subsidies were in average higher than services in Canada during the period before 1987 and, than in the US in some years.

Figure 2.5. Freight moved by rail

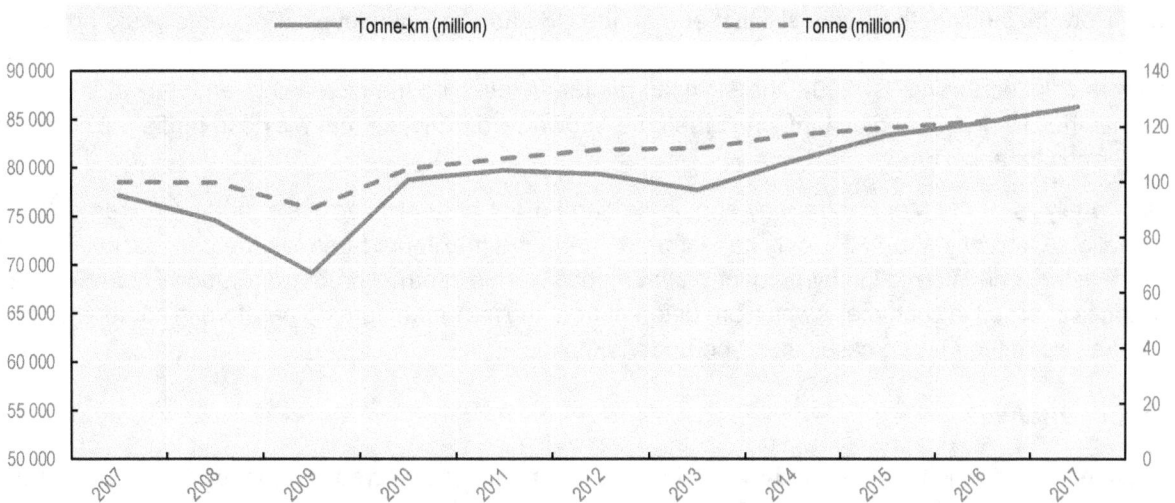

Source: Elaborated by the OECD with data from ARTF (2018[5]), *Anuario Estadístico Ferroviario 2017* [Railway Statistical Yearbook 2017], https://www.gob.mx/artf/acciones-y-programas/anuario-estadistico-ferroviario-2017-152797 (accessed 2 March 2019).

Figure 2.6. Average tariffs of rail freight

2012 USD cents/tonne-km

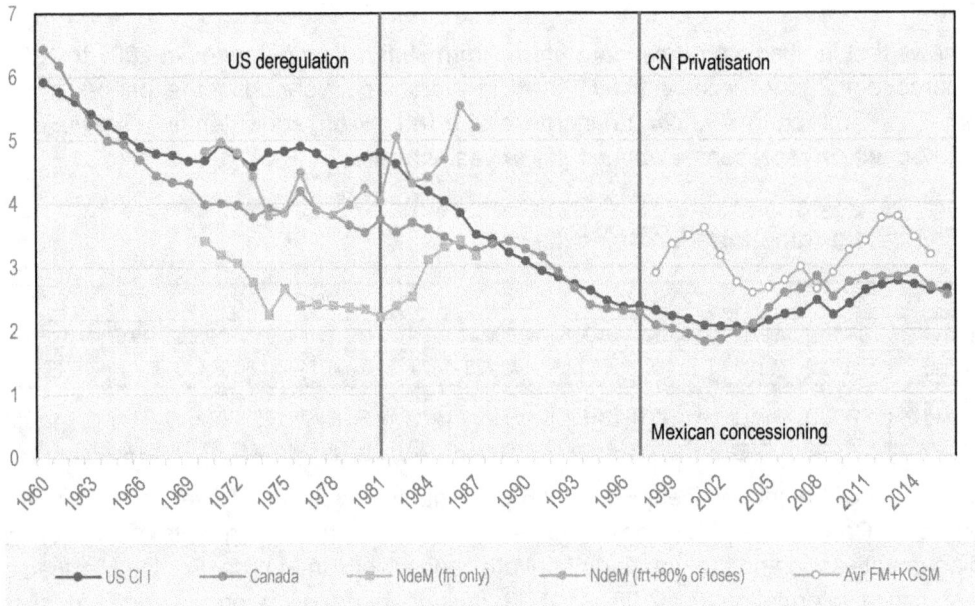

Notes: National Railways of Mexico was composed of three railways: Nacionales de Mexico (NdeM), Ferrocarril Chihuahua-Pacifico (Chepe) and Ferrocarril del Pacifico (FdelP). The data reported here is for NdeM only but representative of FNM given the small scale of FdelP and Chepe operations.
Source: (ITF, 2014[6]), *Freight Railway Development in Mexico*, https://dx.doi.org/10.1787/5jlwvzjd60kb-en, updated to add 2013-16 data based on AAR "Railroad Facts" and US BEA GDP series.

It stands out that Canadian and American rail tariffs had a decreasing path, contrary to the Mexican case that showed an incremental tendency. In 1987, the real Mexican average tariff was 48.5% higher than the American and 67.7% higher than the Canadian.

In the years after the Mexican concession, the national tariffs dropped in comparison with the previous years. Notwithstanding, they were still higher than the US and Canadian levels. For some years however, the Mexican tariffs followed an opposite trend, which contrasts to the American and the Canadian tariffs that were still decreasing. By 2002, the Mexican rail tariffs reversed the increasing tendency at the same time that the US and Canadian tariffs reversed their downward trend, so that Mexican tariffs got closer to the US and Canadian fares.

A tariff analysis of the Mexican railway should be carried out on a regular basis, but it requires detailed information. Currently, the ARFT only has information on the maximum fares, as the concession holders must register such information by product on yearly basis. This information however, does not reflect the real prices charged to costumers, which are different from the maximum fares. Therefore, a comprehensive tariff analysis of the Mexico case cannot be undertaken.

Product analysis

The share of the freight transported by rail by type of product, measured in tonnes, practically did not change for the last 10 years. Table 2.5 presents the tonnes carried by rail and its relative weight with respect to the total freight from 2007 to 2017 as well as the total volume of freight by product. The industrial products went from 48.8 million tonnes in 2007 to 59.8 million in 2017 – a 22.5% increase. The agricultural products grew 22.8% – from 26.3 million to 32.3 million. The mineral products on the other hand, went up about 30.6% and the oil by-products experienced an increase of 120.8%, the most relevant of the period. In contrast, the inorganic goods decreased 1.7% in the ten years.

As can be seen in Table 2.6, the most important products for the rail mode of transport are the industrial-related, as they represent more than 46.0% of the total tonnage for each year – 47.8% in average for the whole period. The second most relevant type of product is agricultural-related, as they accounted between 22.5% (2013) and 27.9% (2009). In addition, the third type are mineral-related, representing between 10.9% (2016) and 14.0% (2013).

It is worth to mention that the three most relevant categories of products carried by rail represented between 84.5% (2014) and 87.6% (2008) of the total tonnage for the period – 85.8% in average. The oil-related products, the fourth in relevance, are those that have changed the most in its proportion, moving from 5.2% in 2008 to 9.2% in 2014 and 2017.

Table 2.5. Rail freight transportation by group product, in tonnes

Million tonnes, yearly

Group of products	2007	2008	2009	2010	2011	2012	2013	2014	2015	2016	2017
Industrial	48.8	47.7	41.7	49.0	50.9	53.4	54.9	56.5	57.6	58.9	59.8
Agricultural	26.3	26.3	25.2	27.0	26.5	26.7	25.2	27.1	29.8	31.8	32.3
Mineral	12.1	13.3	10.9	13.7	15.2	15.4	15.7	15.2	14.7	13.3	15.8
Oil	5.3	5.2	6.4	7.7	8.4	8.7	9.2	10.8	10.7	11.0	11.7
Inorganic	5.9	5.7	4.8	5.6	6.0	5.9	5.4	5.8	5.2	5.5	5.8
Forest	1.1	1.0	0.8	0.9	1.0	1.1	1.1	1.2	1.2	1.1	1.1
Animal	0.4	0.4	0.4	0.5	0.5	0.5	0.4	0.4	0.4	0.4	0.4
Total	99.9	99.6	90.2	104.4	108.5	111.7	111.9	117	119.6	122	126.9

Source: Adapted from ARTF (2018[5]), *Anuario Estadístico Ferroviario 2017* (Railway Statistical Yearbook 2017), https://www.gob.mx/artf/acciones-y-programas/anuario-estadistico-ferroviario-2017-152797 (accessed 31 January 2018).

Table 2.6. Rail freight transportation by group of product

Percentage, yearly

Group of products	2007	2008	2009	2010	2011	2012	2013	2014	2015	2016	2017
Industrial	48.9%	47.8%	46.2%	46.8%	47.0%	47.8%	49.1%	48.3%	48.2%	48.3%	47.1%
Agricultural	26.4%	26.4%	27.9%	25.8%	24.4%	23.9%	22.5%	23.2%	24.9%	26.1%	25.5%
Mineral	12.1%	13.3%	12.1%	13.1%	14.0%	13.8%	14.0%	13.0%	12.3%	10.9%	12.5%
Oil	5.3%	5.2%	7.1%	7.4%	7.7%	7.8%	8.2%	9.2%	8.9%	9.0%	9.2%
Inorganic	5.9%	5.7%	5.3%	5.4%	5.5%	5.3%	4.8%	5.0%	4.3%	4.5%	4.6%
Forest	1.1%	1.0%	0.9%	0.9%	0.9%	1.0%	1.0%	1.0%	1.0%	0.9%	0.9%
Animal	0.4%	0.4%	0.4%	0.5%	0.5%	0.4%	0.4%	0.3%	0.3%	0.3%	0.3%
Total	100%	100%	100%	100%	100%	100%	100%	100%	100%	100%	100%

Source: Adapted from ARTF (2018[5]), *Anuario Estadístico Ferroviario 2017* (Railway Statistical Yearbook 2017), https://www.gob.mx/artf/acciones-y-programas/anuario-estadistico-ferroviario-2017-152797 (accessed 31 January 2018).

Shares of the rail sector

Table 2.7 presents the distribution of the freight between railway firms in Mexico for the fiscal year 2017. From the 126.9 million of tonnes transported in the country, Ferrocarril Mexicano (Ferromex) moved approximately 46.0% (58.3 million) of freight, Kansas Southern of Mexico (KCSM) 33.9% (43.1%) and Ferrosur 14.9% (18.9 million). These three lines concentrated 94.8% of the total freight in 2017. In fact, the consortium Ferromex-Ferrosur accounted for 60.9% of the total tonnage. The remaining four short lines

Coahuila-Durango (LFCD), Ferrocarril y Terminal del Valle de México (Ferrovalle), Ferrocarril del Istmo de Tehuantepec (FIT) and Administradora de la Vía Corta Tijuana-Tecate (Admicarga) accounted for 6.6 million tonnes, which represented 5.2% of the total amount.

Regarding the total tonne-kilometres, Ferromex summed up 45.6 billion tonnes-km, approximately 52.9%; KCSM billed 30.4 billion tonnes-km, which represented 35.2%; and Ferrosur, 8.8 billion tonnes-km, 10.2%. Thus, the three lines had 98.3% of the total of tonne-km during 2017. The four short lines gathered 2% of the share of tonnes-km with 1.5 billion.

Table 2.7. Distribution of the cargo remitted by concessionaires and assignees in Mexico 2017

Concessionaires/ assignees	Tonne		Tonne-km		Loaded cars
	Million	Share	Thousands of million	Share	Number of units
Ferromex	58.3	46.0%	45.6	52.9%	956 591
KCSM	43.1	33.9%	30.4	35.2%	881 880
Ferrosur	18.9	14.9%	8.8	10.2%	279 614
LCD	3.2	2.6%	0.8	0.9%	37 885
FTVM	2.6	2.1%	0.1	0.1%	29 274
FIT**	0.6	0.4%	0.6	0.7%	7 121
ADMICARGA	0.2	0.1%	0.0	0.0%	2 633
TOTAL	126.9	100%	86.3	100%	2 194 998

* Considers the traffic of the railway companies (local and remitted).
** Derived from the modality imposed by the Ministry of Communications and Transports (SCT), the tracks of Chiapas and Mayab were operated by Ferrocarril del Istmo de Tehuantepec (FIT) during 2016.
Source: Adapted from ARTF (2018[5]), *Anuario Estadístico Ferroviario 2017* (Railway Statistical Yearbook 2017), https://www.gob.mx/artf/acciones-y-programas/anuario-estadistico-ferroviario-2017-152797 (accessed 31 January 2018).

Spatial analysis

The main commercial routes for rail freight transportation in Mexico are linked to foreign trade, see Table 2.8. In Mexico, railway transportation of goods – measured as millions of tonnes – has been increasing steadily since 2010. Before 2014, this growth was driven by local transportation of products; however, in 2014 the tendency reversed and the flow of imports through the Mexico-USA border was the main source of progress (ARTF, 2018[5]).

In 2017, the Northeast line (under KCSM management) was the corridor with the greatest traffic density by kilometre – 7.16 million ton-km/km. The former derives from the importance of the Mexico-USA crossing, especially through Piedras Negras, Coahuila and Nuevo Laredo, Tamaulipas. In 2017, terrestrial trade represented 71% of the total international cargo. On the other hand, the most important ports for the rail industry are Veracruz and Manzanillo, which serve the Atlantic and Pacific coast of Mexico, respectively. The two ports accounted for 63% of the 23.2 millions of tonnes that were moved by ship in 2017 (ARTF, 2018[5]).

Figure 2.7. Cargo distribution of freight rail by destination in Mexico

Million tonnes per year

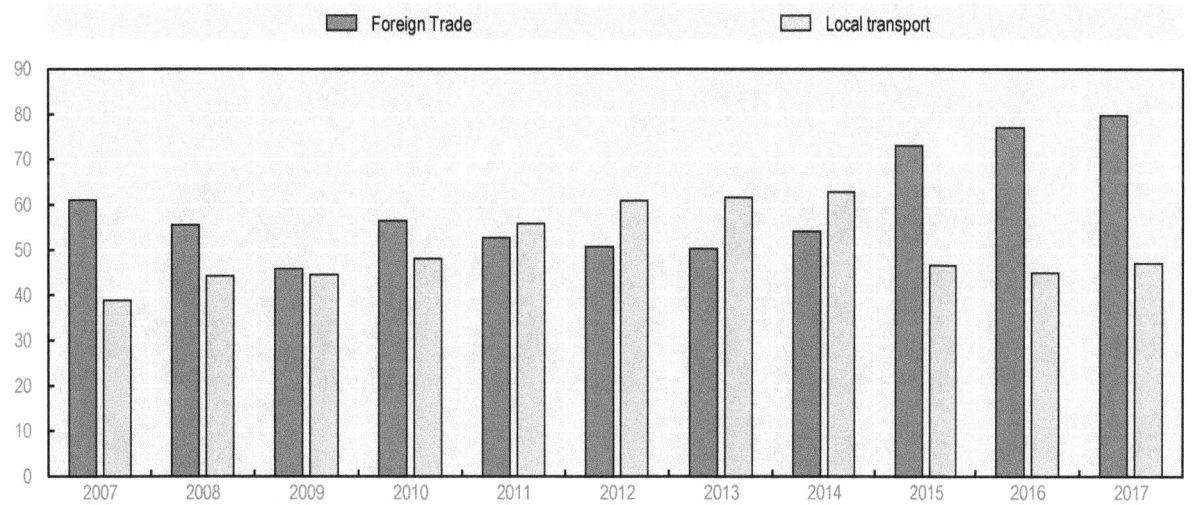

Source: (ARTF, 2018[5]) *Anuario Estadístico Ferroviario 2017* (Railway Statistical Yearbook 2017), https://www.gob.mx/artf/acciones-y-programas/anuario-estadistico-ferroviario-2017-152797 (accessed 31 January 2018).

The impact of the transport industry can be seen in those cities that are relevant from a logistics standpoint. These cities are located in the Mexico-USA border or have important ports, but do not manufacture the transported goods. For example, in the case of Colima and Tamaulipas, activities related to transport, mail and storage accounted for 11% and 10% of their 2017 GDP, respectively (INEGI, 2019[4]). These shares are the highest among all Mexican states and five out of the eight cities considered in Figure 2.8 rank on the top 10% in this indicator.

Garcia Ortega and Martner Pyrelongue (2018[7]) analysed the geographical flow of the rail freight in Mexico using data from 2016. The objective of the research was the identification of freight distribution across the rail network and usage of commercial corridors. The cargo was differentiated between local traffic, interlineal-sent and interlineal in transit. Local traffic refers to the freight moved by one operator or railway firm. In 2016, the local traffic was about 89.2% (109.3 million tonnes) of the total freight in the country (122.4 million). Interlineal sent refers to the freight that is handled by two operators; thus, it passes through a connection node between the network of the origin concession holder and the network of the destination licence – it accounted for 12.7 million and 10.3% of the 2016 total cargo. Finally, the interlineal in transit involves three firms; origin, destination and in-between. This type of cargo accounted for 0.4% with 441 thousands of tonnes.

Table 2.8 shows the total freight according to the type of traffic by firm. The traffic involving more than two rail networks – interlineal in sent traffic – with respect of the total volume is low, only 0.3% of the total traffic. Ferrosur is the line with the largest proportion of its cargo involving more than two rail firms with 215 091 tonnes transported, which represents 29.1% of the total interlineal in transit traffic. Taking interlineal sent traffic and interlineal in transit traffic together, Ferromex is the major player with 4.9 million tonnes transported.

Figure 2.8. Share of international rail cargo by international crossing and port in Mexico

Million tonnes per year

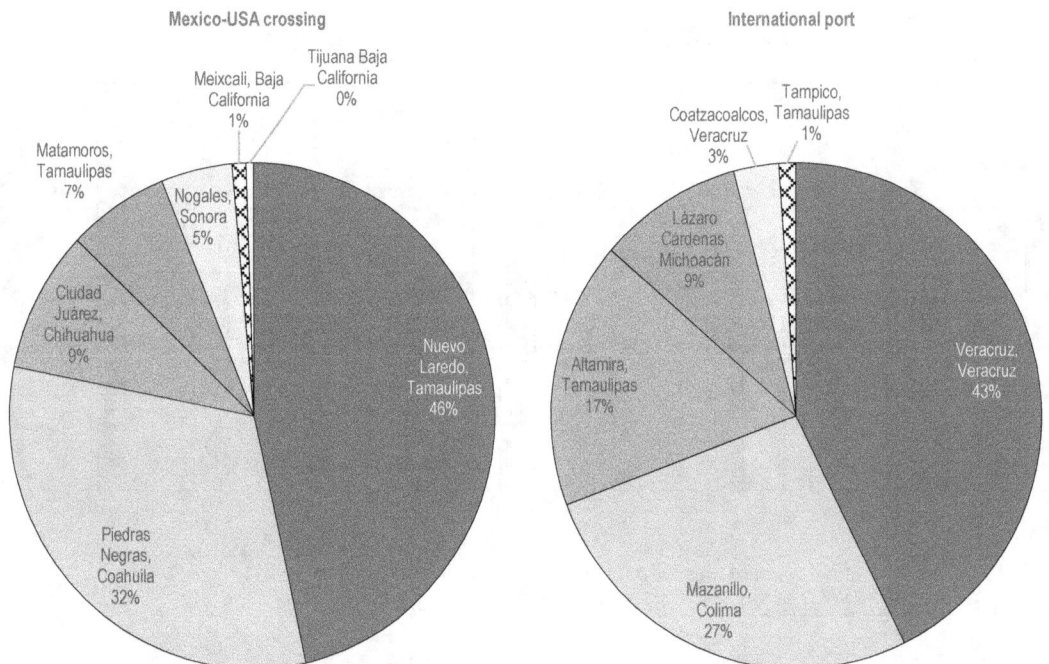

Source: ARTF (2018[5]), *Anuario Estadístico Ferroviario 2017* (Railway Statistical Yearbook 2017), https://www.gob.mx/artf/acciones-y-programas/anuario-estadistico-ferroviario-2017-152797 (accessed 31 January 2018).

Table 2.8. Freight according to the type of traffic in Mexico

Tonnes

Firms	Local traffic	% across type of traffic	Interlineal sent traffic	% across type of traffic	Interlineal in transit traffic	% across type of traffic	Total by firm	% across firms
Ferromex	51 396 044	91.1	4 832 316	8.6	156 377	0.3	56 384 737	46.0
Ferrosur	12 031 841	70.9	4 717 491	27.8	215 091	1.3	16 964 423	13.8
KCSM	39 486 366	94.1	2 376 038	5.6	69 711	0.2	41 932 115	34.2
FIT-CH-M	1 305 227	100	0	0	0	0	1 305 227	1.1
LCD	2 630 544	76.9	787 285	23.0	0	0	3 417 829	2.8
TFVM	2 453 064	100	0	0	0	0	2 453 064	2
Traffic	109 303 085	89.2	12 713 130	10.3	441 179	0.3	122 457 394	100

Source: Reproduction of García Ortega and Martner Pyrelongue (2018[7]), "Análisis Geográfico de los Flujos de Carga Ferroviaria en México con Datos de 2016 [*Geographic Analysis of Rail Freight Flows in Mexico with 2016 Data*]", https://imt.mx/archivos/Publicaciones/PublicacionTecnica/pt521.pdf (accessed 1 March 2019).

Table 2.9 shows the main nodes or terminals for local rail traffic, which in 2016 distributed 109 million tonnes of cargo in Mexico. Garcia Ortega and Martner Pyrelongue (2018[7]) analysed 348 nodes of distribution from the side of the origin and 412 nodes receiving cargo (destination). From these, 25 origin nodes summed up 74% of the total outgoing freight and 27 concentrated 60% of the incoming cargo. As concluded, the integration of the 42 most important origin-destination nodes resumes 78.8% of the outgoing and 62.3% of the incoming cargo. In fact, they also conclude that these 42 nodes are located along the three main commercial rail corridors of México.

1. The Centre - North corridor which connects Mexico City and two border crossings in the United States, Nuevo Laredo in Tamaulipas and Piedras Negras in Coahuila. As it can be seen in the Table 2.9, these are the most important nodes in terms of local traffic.
2. The west transverse corridor connecting the Pacific through the port of Manzanillo and Mexico City.
3. The east transverse corridor connecting the Gulf of Mexico through the port of Veracruz and Mexico City.

Garcia Ortega and Martner Pyrelongue (2018[7]) identified that with few exemptions (Monterrey, Pantaco and Ciudad Frontera) the bigger nodes are located in ports or border crossings. Besides, in these terminals, origin movements were bigger than destinies, as they are imports distributed across the national territory through the main corridors of each concession holders – with the exemption of Guaymas. At the contrary, the inland nodes presented more destination movements.

In summary, the authors concluded that for local traffic, 35% of the total cargo was moved through nine crossing nodes and were related to international trade. Ten more nodes were associated to the production and consumption of the major urban areas and 23 more nodes (19% of the freight) were linked to specialised cargo.

Table 2.10 presents the main nodes with interlineal sent traffic. As mentioned before, in 2016, the cargo handled by two operators summed up 12.6 million tonnes. This freight was distributed through 167 origin nodes and 197 destination terminals. The nodes disclosed in the Table 2.10 however, represented 86.2% and 78.5% of origin and destination nodes.

The authors concluded that this type of cargo is concentrated in the central region of the country. More specifically, the following corridors:

1. Manzanillo – Guadalajara – Cortazar – Queretaro – Bojay
2. Coatzacoalcos – Jaltipan – Tuxtepec – Molino – Panzacola – Puebla
3. Veracruz – Cd. Sahagún – Pantaco – Metepec – Toluca

One third of the cargo was linked to other corridors and cities as Nuevo Laredo, Monterrey, Quimica del Rey and Piedras Negras, which added 12.1% of the interlineal sent traffic.

The most representative nodes with interlineal traffic in transit are listed in the

Table 2.11. From the total cargo involving more than three operators (441 178 tonnes), nine terminals concentrated 92.1% of the total freight in origin movements and ten added 88.3% of the cargo in destination nodes. In general, this type of flow is mostly unidirectional, which implies that terminals with this type of logistics are mainly recipients or issuers. Nonetheless, it stands out that freight traveling across three or more operators is infrequent in Mexico.

In general terms, the local traffic is the most representative on the rail industry as interlineal requires agreements between firms to share infrastructure.

Table 2.9. Main freight nodes for local traffic in Mexico

Nodes	Origin (tonnes)	%	Destination (tonnes)	%	Total (tonnes)
Nuevo Laredo	18 015 349	16.5	4 272 489	3.9	22 287 838
Piedras Negras	10 853 824	9.9	5 735 430	5.2	16 589 254
Monterrey	1 298 643	1.2	8 712 609	8	10 011 251
Veracruz	7 157 720	6.5	674 994	0.6	7 832 713
Lazaro Cardenas	3 853 651	3.5	2 443 357	2.2	6 297 009
Ciudad Juarez	4 473 766	4.1	1 215 833	1.1	5 689 599

Nodes	Origin (tonnes)	%	Destination (tonnes)	%	Total (tonnes)
Pantaco	860 506	0.8	4 661 326	4.3	5 521 831
Manzanillo	4 312 294	3.9	1 173 240	1.1	5 485 534
Cd Frontera	1 147 104	1	4 021 639	3.7	5 168 742
Matamoros	3 609 844	3.3	1 535 084	1.4	5 144 928
Tlalnepantla	446 491	0.4	3 694 152	3.4	4 140 643
Rio Escondido	2 071 409	1.9	1 873 891	1.7	3 945 301
Nogales	2 167 474	2	1 501 419	1.4	3 668 893
Altamira	3 056 726	2.8	230 798	0.2	3 287 524
Guadalajara	389 542	0.4	2 770 727	2.5	3 160 268
San Luis Potosi	314 524	0.3	2 703 095	2.5	3 017 618
Cd Industrial	1 997 730	1.8	767 931	0.7	2 765 662
Cuautitlán	435 664	0.4	2 189 660	2	2 625 324
Guaymas	310 762	0.3	2 131 687	2	2 442 449
Torreon	879 558	0.8	1 351 935	1.2	2 231 493
Minatitlan	2 191 878	2	0	0	2 191 878
San Juan De Los Lagos	11 068	0	2 136 102	2	2 147 169
Tecoman	2 031 214	1.9	10	0	2 031 224
Huehuetoca	1 875 512	1.7	27 331	0	1 902 843
Silao	1 259 380	1.2	608 107	0.6	1 867 488
Salinas Victoria	440 240	0.4	1 397 478	1.3	1 837 717
Tula	1 396 670	1.3	288 070	0.3	1 684 740
San Juan Del Rio	24 848	0	1 555 312	1.4	1 580 160
Moyotzingo	0	0	1 521 295	1.4	1 521 295
El Castillo	46 112	0	1 381 244	1.3	1 427 357
Tepeaca	1 280 543	1.2	93 648	0.1	1 374 191
Lecheria	161 219	0.1	1 124 693	1	1 285 913
Gómez Palacio	14 675	0	1 231 947	1.1	1 246 622
Zapotiltic	1 112 430	1	127 709	0.1	1 240 139
Querétaro	5 250	0	1 217 747	1.1	1 222 997
Las Palmas	1 110 720	1	104 237	0.1	1 214 957
Pedro C. Morales	1 190 880	1.1	20 813	0	1 211 693
Cananea	1 173 489	1.1	18 693	0	1 192 182
Ahorcado	219	0	1 168 856	1.1	1 169 075
Tamuin	0	0	1 070 317	1	1 070 317
Palau	1 044 125	1	565	0	1 044 690
Tampico	1 001 459	0.9	27 105	0	1 028 564
Subtotal	85 024 512	77.8	68 782 574	62.9	153 807 086
Total	109 303 085	100	109 303 085	100	

Source: García Ortega and Martner Pyrelongue (2018[7]), "Análisis Geográfico de los Flujos de Carga Ferroviaria en México con Datos de 2016 (Geographic Analysis of Rail Freight Flows in Mexico with 2016 Data)", https://imt.mx/archivos/Publicaciones/PublicacionTecnica/pt521.pdf (accessed 1 March 2019).

Table 2.10. Interlineal sent traffic in Mexico

Nodes	Origin (tonnes)	%	Destination (tonnes)	%	Total (tonnes)
Veracruz	1 293 508	10.3	292 137	2.3	1 585 645
Xoxtla	181 694	1.4	1 205 009	9.6	1 386 703
Cortazar	360 983	2.9	877 576	7.0	1 238 559
Ing A Lira Arciniega	376 668	3.0	813 584	6.5	1 190 252
Nuevo Laredo	757 839	6.0	301 875	2.4	1 059 713
Bojay	582 054	4.6	430 027	3.4	1 012 081
Queretaro	48 872	0.4	711 043	5.6	759 915

Nodes	Origin (tonnes)	%	Destination (tonnes)	%	Total (tonnes)
Manzanillo	726 839	5.8	227	0.002	727 066
Quimica del Rey	713 859	5.7	1 735	0.01	715 593
Piedras Negras	369 456	2.9	329 576	2.6	699 032
Jaltipan	584 429	4.6	34 601	0.3	619 029
Monterrey	261 937	2.1	320 547	2.5	582 484
Guanomex	549 731	4.4	1 577	0.01	551 308
Coatzacoalcos	369 284	2.9	68 744	0.5	438 028
Puebla	118 744	0.9	311 431	2.5	430 175
Salamanca	364 452	2.9	62 685	0.5	427 137
Tecoman	421 774	3.3	0	0.0	421 774
Lazaro Cardenas	363 977	2.9	32 739	0.3	396 716
Guadalajara	6 982	0.1	384 334	3.0	391 316
Ciudad Juarez	214 706	1.7	166 471	1.3	381 177
Kmb170	377 899	3.0	0	0.0	377 899
Morelia	60	0.0005	358 977	2.8	359 037
San Luis Potosi	84 956	0.7	259 132	2.1	344 087
Panzacola	213 356	1.7	89 637	0.7	302 993
Molino	44 534	0.4	245 217	1.9	289 752
Pantaco	0	0.0	271 164	2.2	271 164
Durango	33 586	0.3	215 122	1.7	248 708
San Juan del Rio	208 457	1.7	33 693	0.3	242 150
Xalostoc	2 504	0.02	237 260	1.9	239 764
Altamira	227 151	1.8	6 425	0.1	233 576
Guasave	202 232	1.6	0	0.0	202 232
Paula	5 278	0.04	194 876	1.5	200 154
Metepec	0	0.0	184 471	1.5	184 471
Tres Valles	62 610	0.5	108 457	0.9	171 067
Toluca	468	0.0	166 465	1.3	166 933
Cd Frontera	5 392	0.04	159 948	1.3	165 341
Cangrejera	144 236	1.1	19 608	0.2	163 845
Cd Sahagun	121 892	1.0	40 808	0.3	162 700
La Junta	36 919	0.3	111 670	0.9	148 588
Pedro C. Morales	147 208	1.2	600	0.005	147 808
Centauro	22 806	0.2	114 911	0.9	137 717
Tuxtepec	102 969	0.8	30 818	0.2	133 788
Víctor Rosales	13 318	0.1	118 628	0.9	131 947
Rio Escondido	0	0.0	128 088	1.0	128 088
Vito	22 974	0.2	104 327	0.8	127 301
Pabellon	0	0.0	126 796	1.0	126 796
Gomez Palacio	119 626	0.9	2 358	0.02	121 984
Apaseo	0	0.0	113 116	0.9	113 116
Tlacote	1 566	0.01	100 906	0.8	102 472
Subtotal	10 869 786	86.2	9 889 394	78.5	20 759 180
Tota	12 605 135		12 605 135		

Source: García Ortega and Martner Pyrelongue (2018[7]), "Análisis Geográfico de los Flujos de Carga Ferroviaria en México con Datos de 2016 (Geographic Analysis of Rail Freight Flows in Mexico with 2016 Data)", https://imt.mx/archivos/Publicaciones/PublicacionTecnica/pt521.pdf (accessed 1 March 2019).

Table 2.11. Interlineal traffic in transit in Mexico

Nodes	Origin (tonnes)	%	Destination (tonnes)	%	Total (tonnes)
Cortazar	101 768	23.1	19 917	4.5	121 684
Mérida	19 572	4.4	97 987	22.2	117 559
Quimica del Rey	75 674	17.2	449	0.1	76 123
Ing. A Lira Arciniega	67 371	15.3	0	0	67 371
Miramar	0	0	63 326	14.4	63 326
Toluca	449	0.1	60 161	13.6	60 610
Coatzacoalcos	51 192	11.6	0	0	51 192
Ing. Roberto Ayala	370	0.1	47 554	10.8	47 924
Bajio	32 606	7.4	0	0	32 606
Veracruz	0	0	32 606	7.4	32 606
Durango	4 405	1	16 095	3.6	20 501
Vito	19 138	4.3	0	0	19 138
San Juan Del Río	0	0	18 860	4.3	18 860
Lazaro Cardenas	17 572	4	0	0	17 572
Arriaga	0	0	16 464	3.7	16 464
Centauro	16 244	3.7	0	0	16 244
Temascalapa	0	0	16 190	3.7	16 190
Subtotal	406 362	92.1	389 610	88.3	795 971
Total	441 178		441 178		

Source: García Ortega and Martner Pyrelongue (2018[7]), "Análisis Geográfico de los Flujos de Carga Ferroviaria en México con Datos de 2016 (Geographic Analysis of Rail Freight Flows in Mexico with 2016 Data)", https://imt.mx/archivos/Publicaciones/PublicacionTecnica/pt521.pdf (accessed 1 March 2019).

International Comparison

In Mexico, freight transportation by railways represents 25% of the total terrestrial cargo – while the OECD's average is of 38% (ITF, 2018[8]). Although the country's use of railways is close to the average use in OECD member countries, it lags behind in density of rail lines. Mexico has 1.37 km of rail lines *per* 100 sq.km (Figure 2.9) (ITF, 2018[8]). The scarce coverage of rail lines makes road transportation particularly attractive, as in some areas of the country it is the only option available (ITF, 2018[8]).

The use of railways is mainly determined by the type of products that are transported and the distance covered. For example, in the United States an important share of the freight transportation by rail is determined by the large volumes of bulk commodities that are carried over long distances. In line with the previous statement, and according to the ITF, approximately 80% of the world cargo transportation by rail is done in three countries: People's Republic of China, Russian Federation and the United States (OECD and IFT, 2017[9]).

There is a strong correlation between a country's GDP growth and its use of railways – particularly as rails are mainly used to carry out commodities (OECD and IFT, 2017[9]). Nonetheless, as the value of goods produced increases, products are more likely to be transported by road instead of freight, largely reflecting changes in product mix as a country's economy grows.

Figure 2.9. Rail lines density

Km per 100 km²

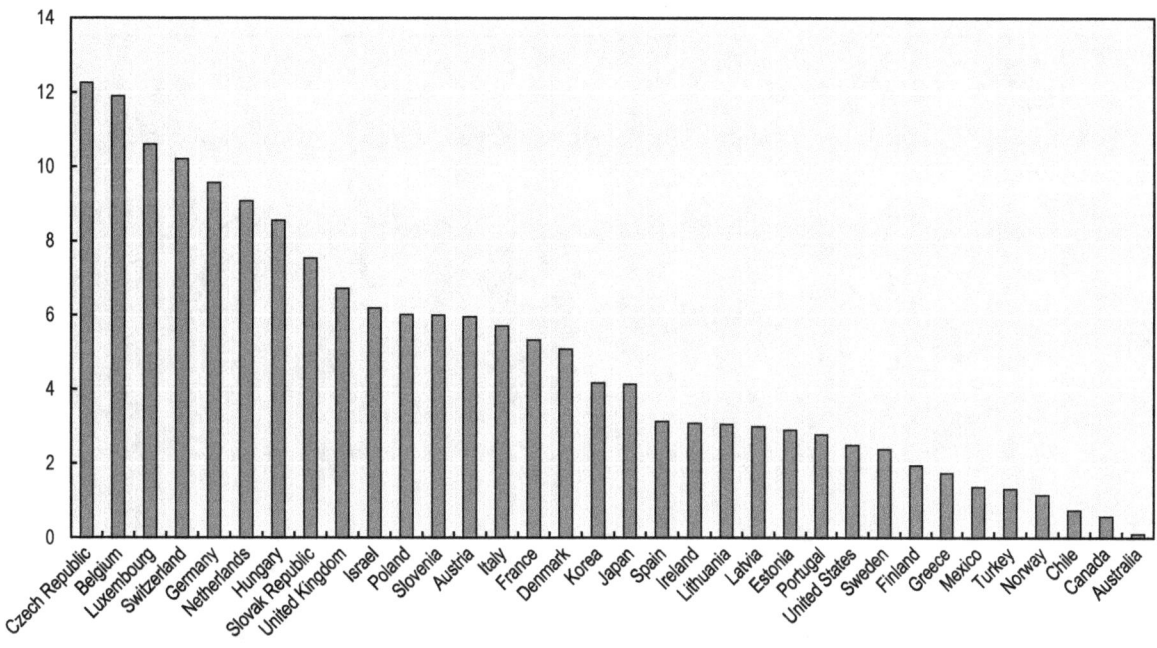

Source: (ITF, 2018[8]), *ITF Transport Statistics-Goods Transport*, http://dx.doi.org/10.1787/trsprt-data-en.

It is worth mentioning that growth and investment in rail transportation have been sustained in Mexico and growth trends after restructuring have been favourable in comparison to earlier periods and, to a degree, in comparison to the USA (see Figure 2.10). Moreover, after the private concessions were introduced, the rail tonne-km in Mexico has grown at a faster rate than the GDP. The former implies that the share and importance of the rail sector for the Mexican economy has increased in the last years.

In 2011-2013, the average elasticity of global trade to GDP was 1.4, meaning that foreign trade increases 1.4% for every 1% increase in GDP (OECD and IFT, 2017[9]). Given that Mexico's share of freight that is destined to the USA and foreign markets has been increasing, the country is most likely to benefit from a global economy.

Figure 2.10. Rail tonne-km vs GDP

Index 1998=100

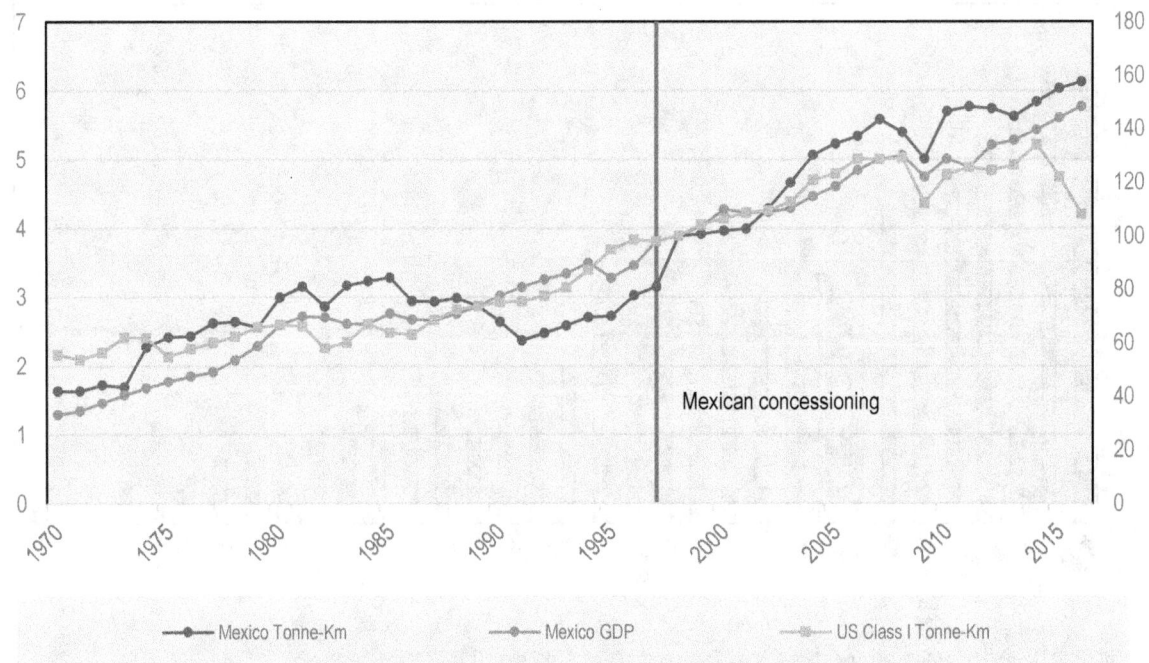

Source: (STB, 2018[10]), *Statistics of Class 1 Freight Railroads*, Surface Transportation Board, Washington DC, https://www.stb.gov/Econdata.nsf/M%20Statistics%20of%20Class%201%20Feight%20RR?OpenPage (accessed 5 March 2019); ARTF (2018[5]), *Anuario Estadístico Ferroviario 2017* (Railway Statistical Yearbook 2017), https://www.gob.mx/artf/acciones-y-programas/anuario-estadistico-ferroviario-2017-152797 (accessed 31 January 2018).

Nonetheless, Mexico's investment in rail infrastructure has been low in comparison to other OECD countries (Figure 2.11). The increase in the freight transported by train is a consequence of the growth in the amount of goods transported, instead of a rise in the kilometers of the rail lines available. Current concession titles do not require companies to make investments in the rail infrastructure; however, some companies have invested in by-passes or other infrastructure projects in exchange of an increase in their exclusivity rights (see Chapter 2 for further details). For example, Ferromex was awarded five more years of exclusivity as exchange for building the Celaya bypass.

Most of the existing railway lines were built during the 20th century and many of the areas where a potential line could build are already invaded. In this sense, critical infrastructure investments are required to improve the scope of the railway in Mexico.

It is important to point out that critical infrastructure investments are needed in areas related to security. In meetings with private stakeholders, concessionaires and members of the chambers representing the users, mentioned the need of investing in boom barriers, as in many cases the train lines pass through cities or congested streets. Moreover, the little investment has been devoted to the rehabilitation of the rail lines, as recently accidents have occurred in segments of the line where trains drive at 10-15 km/h.

Figure 2.11. Rail infrastructure investment as % of GDP

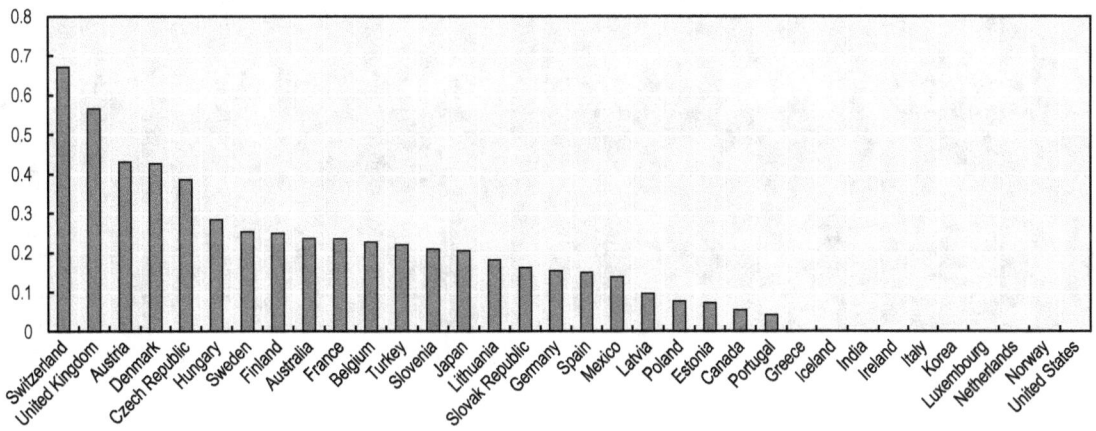

Source: ITF (2018[8]), *ITF Transport Statistics-Goods Transport*, http://dx.doi.org/10.1787/trsprt-data-en.

References

ARTF (2018), *Anuario Estadístico Ferroviario 2017 [Railway Statistical Yearbook 2017]*, SCT, https://www.gob.mx/artf/acciones-y-programas/anuario-estadistico-ferroviario-2017-152797. [5]

García Ortega, G. and C. Martner Pyrelongue (2018), "Análisis Geográfico de los Flujos de Carga Ferroviaria en México con Datos de 2016 [Geographic Analysis of Rail Freight Flows in Mexico with 2016 Data]", No. 521, Instituto Mexicano del Transporte, Sanfandilla, Querétaro, https://imt.mx/archivos/Publicaciones/PublicacionTecnica/pt521.pdf (accessed on 1 March 2019). [7]

Gobierno de México (2019), *Instituto Mexicano del Transporte [Mexican Transport Institute]*, Querétaro, https://www.gob.mx/imt (accessed on 5 March 2019). [3]

INEGI (2019), *Banco de Información Económica (BIE) [Economic Information Bank]*, https://www.inegi.org.mx/sistemas/bie/ (accessed on 5 March 2019). [4]

INEGI (n.d.), *PIB y cuentas nacionales*, https://www.inegi.org.mx/temas/pib/ (accessed on 1 June 2019). [2]

ITF (2018), *ITF Transport Statistics-Goods Transport*, http://dx.doi.org/10.1787/trsprt-data-en. [8]

ITF (2014), *Freight Railway Development in Mexico*, OECD Publishing, Paris, https://dx.doi.org/10.1787/5jlwvzjd60kb-en. [6]

OECD and IFT (2017), *ITF Transport Outlook 2017*, https://doi.org/10.1787/25202367. [9]

SCT (2018), *Estadística Básica 2017 [Basic Statistics 2017]*, http://www.sct.gob.mx/transporte-y-medicina-preventiva/autotransporte-federal/estadistica/2017/ (accessed on 5 March 2019). [1]

STB (2018), *Statistics of Class 1 Freight Railroads*, Surface Transportation Board, Washington DC, https://www.stb.gov/Econdata.nsf/M%20Statistics%20of%20Class%201%20Feight%20RR?OpenPage (accessed on 5 March 2019). [10]

3 State of play and reforms of the rail sector of Mexico

This section starts with a brief description of the industry development since its origins. A review of the main characteristics of the current regulatory framework is then presented. In particular, the analysis focuses on the network and competition conditions, exclusivity of the concessions, tariffs schemes and other topics on economic regulation. Finally, examples of best practices regarding regulatory frameworks of the rail industry in the United States and Canada are presented.

Development of railways from the 19th century to 1994

Mexico's first major rail line was inaugurated in 1873, a freight and passenger railway connecting Mexico City to the port of Veracruz on the Gulf of Mexico. The line was financed with British capital by the Mexican Railway Company Limited (*Ferrocarril Mexicano*, which is also the official name of today's Ferromex freight operator that holds concessions on other parts of the network). Under the terms of the concession, granted by the Imperial Government in 1864, the company was given an annual subsidy to operate the line for a period of 25 years. Tariffs for both freight and passenger services were subject to review by the government every two years. The railway was profitable but only moderately so, paying dividends from 1902. It was extensively damaged between 1914 and 1919 during the Mexican revolution and occupation of the port by US troops (Donly, 1920[1]).

In the 1880s, three railways were constructed to serve the central plateau and north of the country, under concessions that provided subsidies for construction of the lines and 10 year periods of freedom from competition from new rail concessions. These three railways were as follows (the locations mentioned are indicated on Figure 3.1, Figure 3.2 and Figure 3.3).

- The Mexican National Railroad (Ferrocarril Nacional), from Mexico City to the north east, via San Luis de Potosi and Saltillo and Monterrey to Laredo on the US border.
- The Mexican Central Railway (Ferrocarril Central Mexicano) with a line from Mexico City to Leon later consolidated with further concessions. These are: 1) one line to El Paso on the US border, 2) a branch to Manzanillo on the Pacific coast through Guadalajara and 3) two branches to the port of Tampico on the Gulf coast, one from Aguascalientes via San Luis Potosi and the other from Torreon via Monterrey.
- The Mexican International Railroad (Ferrocarril Internacional Mexicano), from the Piedras Negras – Eagle Pass crossing on the US border to Torreon on the Central line and to the mining area of Durango in the centre-west.

The concession conditions covered free carriage of mail and military equipment and concessionary passenger tariffs for government officials and military personnel. General tariffs were subject to review by the Ministry of Communications and Public Works every three years (Donly, 1920[1]).

After several failed concession agreements, the Tehuantepec National Railway in the south of the country was built between 1892 and 1894 from the Gulf of Mexico to the Pacific Ocean across the Isthmus of Tehuantepec under concession to an American partnership. On completion, the concession was bought-out and made part of an agreement with a British firm to develop ports on both coasts. The railway operated successfully, carrying Hawaiian sugar and Canadian and US west coast produce to Atlantic ports, despite strong competition from the Panama Canal, until it was extensively damaged in 1913 during the revolution (Donly, 1920[1]).

The Inter-Oceanic Railway (Ferrocarril Interoceanico) was granted a concession to run from Veracruz to Acapulco on the Pacific coast in 1878 and finally opened a line from Veracruz as far as Mexico City in 1891. The Veracruz – Isthmus Railway (Ferrocarril de Verarcruz al Istmo) was granted a concession in 1891 and linked the Mexican Railway at Cordoba to the Tehuantepec National Railway in the south east. The Pan-American Railway (Ferrrocarril Pan-Americano) was granted a concession in 1901 to run along the Pacific coast from the Tehuantepec National Railway to the border with Guatemala (Bach, 1939[2]).

In 1903, the Finance Minister of President Porfirio Diaz began a policy of taking railways into State control in the national strategic and defence interest, acquiring a controlling government share in the Mexican National Railroad. In 1908 this was merged with a series of main line, short line and narrow gauge railways across the country, creating the company Ferrocarriles Nacionales de Mexico (FNM) in 1909, to exercise control on the main trunk lines through majority share ownership (Donly, 1920[1]).

Between 1929 and 1937 the State took majority control of the rest of Mexico's railways. The private holdings in FNM were expropriated in 1937 in an uncontested nationalisation of a system from which the private owners no longer expected to generate profits (Bach, 1939[2]). Five State-owned regional railways were consolidated into FNM in 1987, which was then legally composed of three railways: Nacionales de Mexico (NdeM), the major part, Ferrocarril Chihuahua-Pacifico (Chepe) and Ferrocarril del Pacifico (FdelP).

By the early 1990s, Mexico was experiencing a railroad problem similar to that in other major countries in Latin America. FNM offered poor service, was not very productive and had a deficit of more than half a billion US dollars annually. The government's response, similar to that followed in Argentina and Brazil, was to break FNM into separate pieces and offer them as concessions to be operated by the private sector. The strategy was agreed by an Inter-ministerial Commission on Restructuring established in 1995 (Gobierno de México, 1995[3]), based on a government review that considered a range of options for reform of the rail sector. The government made its first priority facilitating investment in the railway from the private sector as the public sector was not in a position to provide the funding needed (COFECE, 2016[4]).

1995 Law on the Regulation of Rail Services and Mexico's Railway Concessions

Railway concessions

In 1995, the government reformed Mexico's railways by statute through the Law on the Regulation of Rail Services. This provided for the national rail network to be divided into a small number of exclusive, vertically integrated freight railway concessions. The statute gives primary regulatory responsibility to the Ministry of Communications and Transport (SCT). Specific powers concerning rail tariffs and issues of competition are also given to the independent Federal Commission of Economic Competition of Mexico (COFECE). The law is supplemented with more detailed provisions in regulations by the Bylaw on Rail Services issued by the Ministry in 2010, updated in 2011 and 2016.

The 1995 law authorises SCT to grant concessions to private companies to operate rail lines under conditions established by the Ministry and set out in the concession titles. Terms of access to rail infrastructure are established by the three instruments – the law, the bylaw and the concession title agreements – together. The concession titles carry the most practical import; see for example the title document for the Northeast concession, the first to be issued (SCT, 1997[5]). The concessions were issued between 1997 and 1999 and all follow the same format, with some variation in the contents of their clauses. The law limits the initial terms of concessions to 50 years, with the possibility of extension for a maximum of a further 50 years (Allen, 2001[6]).

The concessions were designed to maximise the income produced by sale of the leases and therefore provided long periods of exclusive access to markets. The three main concession titles set exclusive periods for the operation of freight services on the lines under concession, initially for 30 years. The sales yielded approximately USD 3 billion (in 2014 prices). Competition between the concessions to serve Mexico City, Monterrey and the port of Veracruz was created in the structure of the networks under concession.

Some limited trackage and haulage rights were also included in the concession deeds, some to provide for competition, most for more practical operational reasons. Most are limited to specific products, routes, slots and origin-destination pairs (excluding transport between intermediate points). Table 3.3 below, summarises the rights incorporated in one of the concessions agreements, giving an indication of the range of purposes the rights were established to serve. In some cases, they allow specific industrial plants to be reached by two concessions using each other's tracks so that, for example, a single rail operator can serve all of the company's plants. In other cases, they provide access to an industrial park or zone to alternative concessions, sometimes with mention of the explicit goal of fostering competition between the concessions. A few of these concern long segments of trunk lines, others concern access to adjacent freight yards, in some cases they simply provide for switching services for the last leg of interline traffic. Some of the rights ensure connection with US railways through yards at border crossing points. Some of the rights provide temporary relief from congestion on trunk lines, or temporary access to facilities that the second concession is expected to replicate.

In three cases, trackage rights were included in concession titles to provide rights to interconnect isolated lines held by one concession over the lines of another concession. Over the Isthmus of Tehuantepec railway in the south of the country, general access rights were provided for the two neighbouring concessions to run services over its line.

The limited nature of most of the mandated trackage rights was designed to protect the overall market of each concession and maximise its value. The concessions are also allowed to use trackage rights on a voluntary basis to manage disruptions and congested sections of track (Regulation 107).

The government decided to restructure the national rail network into three large, regionally distinct networks of trunk lines with a shared terminal railway for the Mexico City metropolitan region (SCT, 1997[5]). The three main concessions are the Northeast, North-Pacific and Southeast, established by orders issued by the Government (Gobierno de Mexico, 1996[7]). Despite the geographic concentration of assets, the concessions do not give rights to a geographic territory but just to the designated network, and the networks overlap. Seven smaller freight concessions were established on lines with low traffic levels, three of which were awarded to the main concession holders. The concessions were awarded between 1996 and 1999 and transfer to the new operators began in 1997 and was completed in 1999 (ITF, 2014[8]).

The three major concessions were awarded as follows.

- The Northeast line, let to Kansas City Southern of Mexico (KCSM), initially Transportación Ferroviaria Mexicana (TFM), operating the so-called "*golden line*" from Mexico City to Saltillo, Monterrey and the US border at Nuevo Laredo, together with lines to the Gulf ports of Veracruz and Tampico and the Pacific port of Lazaro Cardenas. The concession accounted for 19% of the national network's route kilometres but over 40% of the freight tonne-km carried, and sold for USD 1.4 billion in June 1997 (Allen, 2001[6]). TFM also agreed to pay 0.5% of net operating income to the government in each of the first 15 years and 1.5% for the remainder of the concession (Railway Gazette, 1997[9]). TFM was a consortium of Mexico's biggest maritime shipping company, Transportación Marítima Mexicana (TMM) and Kansas City Southern Industries, which bought out TMM in 2005.

- Ferrocarril Mexicano (Ferromex) purchased the North-Pacific concession in late 1997, covering the Pacific coast and central routes from Mexico City to five US border crossings, with connecting lines from Torreon via Monterrey to the Gulf port of Altamira and from Guadalajara to the Pacific port of Manzanillo. Four other Pacific ports are served by the coastal mainline. Ferromex operates over the largest part of Mexico's rail network. The company is a subsidiary of the mining consortium, Grupo México, Mexico's largest company, and Union Pacific railway, which holds a 26% share. The concession sold for a little under half the value of the Northeast concession, see Table 3.1. Ferromex also purchased two smaller freight concessions: the Ojinaga-Topolobampo concession running from the US border to the Pacific coast and crossing Ferromex two north-south trunk lines; and the Nacozari concession connecting a mine in Sonora to Ferromex US border crossing point at El Paso. It also holds a concession in the northwest running mainly passenger services for tourists, the named "*El Chepe*" line through Copper Canyon between Chihuahua and Los Mochis. Ferromex also operates the Tequila Express passenger service, mainly for tourists, from Guadalajara to Amatitan.

- Ferrosur purchased the Southeast concession and the South short line concession in 1998, operating lines from Mexico City south to the Gulf ports of Veracruz and Coatzacoalcos. Ferrosur is a consortium of banking and industrial interests and was acquired by Ferromex for USD 245 million in stock in 2005 (see section on Mergers and Acquisitions below). Ferrosur was awarded the Oaxaca and Sur concession in 2005, but by 2008 found part of the line uneconomic. SCT took the concession back into State ownership in 2012 and it was awarded to the Isthmus of Tehuantepec railway in 2018.

Access to the metropolitan area of Mexico City and the surrounding Mexico Valley is provided by a neutral track access and terminal company, Ferrocarril y Terminal del Valle de México (Ferrovalle), jointly owned by KCSM, Ferromex, Ferrosur and the government. This also accommodates a commuter passenger operator, the Suburban Railway of the Valley of Mexico Metropolitan Area, given in concession to Construcciones y Auxiliar de Ferrocarriles S.A (CAF) in 2005.

The smaller freight railways are as follows.

- Linea Coahuila-Durango (LFCD) in the centre and north serving steel plants and mines *inter alia*. The concession was purchased in 1998 by steel and mining interests including Altos Hornos de México and Peñoles and is now controlled by Industriales Peñoles. Operation of the lines is contracted to Genesee and Wyoming Railroad (Middleton, Smerk and Diehl, 2007[10]).

- The Isthmus of Tehuantepec railway (FIT) in the south, linking the small Pacific port of Salina de Cruz to the Ferrosur network at Medias Aguas (100 km south of the Gulf Port of Coatzacoalcos). This is a Federal State-owned railway, established in 1999. It does not operate trains itself but provides general trackage rights to other operators, mainly Ferrosur. Operations were initially leased to the Compañía de Ferrocarriles Chiapas-Mayab (FCCM) concession but switched to Ferrosur in 2007.

- The FCCM concession was awarded in 1999, with one line along the Pacific coast of Chiapas from close to the small Pacific port of Salina Cruz to Guatemala and another from the oil refinery at the Gulf port of Coatzacoalcos to the Yucatan peninsula. The concession includes trackage rights to use the Ferrosur and Isthmus lines between Coatzacoalcos and Salinas de Cruz (via Medias Aguas). The concession was bought by Genesee and Wyoming Railroad, sold to Viabilis Holdings in 2008 and taken back by the State in 2016.

- The Via Corta Tijuana-Tecate, which runs 50 km between the cities of Tijuana and Tecate on the border with California. The railway is owned by the State of Baja California and operated by Administradora de la vía corta Tijuana Tecate (Admicarga), which has plans to establish a new line to the port of Ensenada.

Figure 3.1. The initial concession structure in Mexico

Source: (SCT, 2015[11]), *Anuario Estadístico Sector Comunicaciones y Transportes 2014* (2014 Statistical Yearbook of the Communications and Transport Sector), http://www.sct.gob.mx/fileadmin/DireccionesGrales/DGP/estadistica/Anuarios/Anuario_2014.pdf (accessed 3 March 2019).

Table 3.1. Sale prices for the main concessions in Mexico

Concession	Length of rights of way (km)	Amount (Current MXN, year of sale)
Northeast	4 251	11 669 161 355
North-Pacific	6 858	5 075 918 879
Southeast and Via Corta del Sur (Ferrosur)	1 479	3 573 305 106
FERROVALLE	-	177 349 971
Coahuila and Durango	974	180 000 000
Isthmus of Tehuantepec	207	627

Source: COFECE (2016[4]), *Reporte Preliminar sobre Competencia Efectiva en el Sistema Ferroviario Mexicano* (Preliminary report on the Effective Competition in the Mexican Railway System).

The principle mandatory trackage rights that were designated in the annexes to the concession titles to facilitate interconnection are listed in Figure 3.2, with the total number of access rights designated between the concessions listed in Table 3.4, in the section below.

Some of the rights designed to promote interconnection were implemented without delay, serving specific industry plants or connecting fragmented networks (the case of Durango-Coahuila and Chiapas-Mayab). However, there were stalled negotiations between concessions on terms of use for many of the rights. The most significant of these stalled mandatory trackage rights were for KCSM to use Ferromex tracks from Mariscala (near Queretaro) to Guadalajara (Mexico's second city) and to give Ferromex access to KCSM's Viborillas to Ramos Arizpe segment on the main line north to the industrial and commercial centres of

Saltillo and Monterrey. Negotiations over implementation of these rights were protracted and were not settled until 2011, in the context of the acquisition of Ferrosur by Grupo Mexico, owner of Ferromex.

Figure 3.2. Principle mandatory trackage rights specified in concession titles

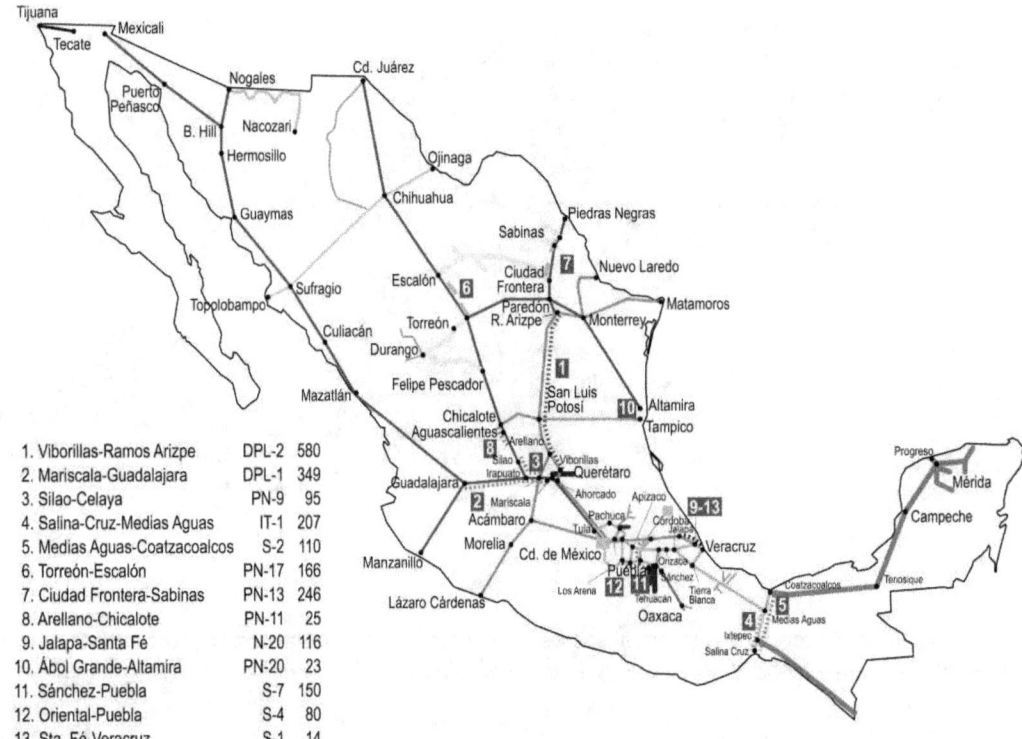

Source: ARTF (2018[12]), *Anuario Estadístico Ferroviario 2017* (Railway Statistical Yearbook 2017), https://www.gob.mx/artf/acciones-y-programas/anuario-estadistico-ferroviario-2017-152797 (accessed 31 January 2018).

Mergers and acquisitions

Grupo Mexico initially proposed acquiring Ferrosur in 2002 but the take-over was rejected by COFECE. In 2005, Grupo Mexico purchased Ferrosur for USD 300 million but the acquisition was opposed by KCSM and in 2006, COFECE ruled against the purchase. The decision was appealed and the acquisition finally permitted to go ahead by a tribunal in 2011, with Ferromex and KCSM agreeing to terms for the exercise of access rights on critical sections of track paving the way for approval. These rights provide, for example, for the Honda car plant in Celaya, between Queretaro and Guadalajara, to be served by KCSM over a short stretch of Ferromex track. Grupo Mexico owns both concessions but Ferromex and Ferrosur retain their separate identities (and the concessions themselves remain separate). During the same period, KCSM was permitted to buy out the other investors in TFM and it is now the primary owner of the concession. As a result, Mexico now effectively has two large rail freight companies – KCSM and Ferromex/Ferrosur – along with the smaller concessions.

Following extensive hurricane damage to the Chiapas line in 2005, Genesee and Wyoming ceased operations and proposed returning the Chiapas-Mayab concession to State ownership in 2007. This was rejected by the SCT, which charged the Isthmus railway with operation of the lines. The concession was sold to Viabilis Holding in 2008 and the length of the concession extended from 30 to 50 years in view of the investment required for rebuilding the Chiapas line, and the exclusivity of the concession rights extended from 18 to 30 years. Viabilis' licence was rescinded in 2016, however, returning the concession to the State. The Isthmus and Chiapas-Mayab lines are important to plans for the development of the southeast, Mexico's poorest region. In 2018, the government integrated the Chiapas-Mayab railway and the Oaxaca y Sur concession into the Isthmus of Tehuantepec concession (Figure 3.3). This includes the general trackage rights to the 100 km of Ferrosur line linking the Isthmus railway from Medias Aguas to Coatzocoalcos (Gobierno de Mexico, 2018[13]).

Figure 3.3. Mexico's rail concessions and short lines in 2018

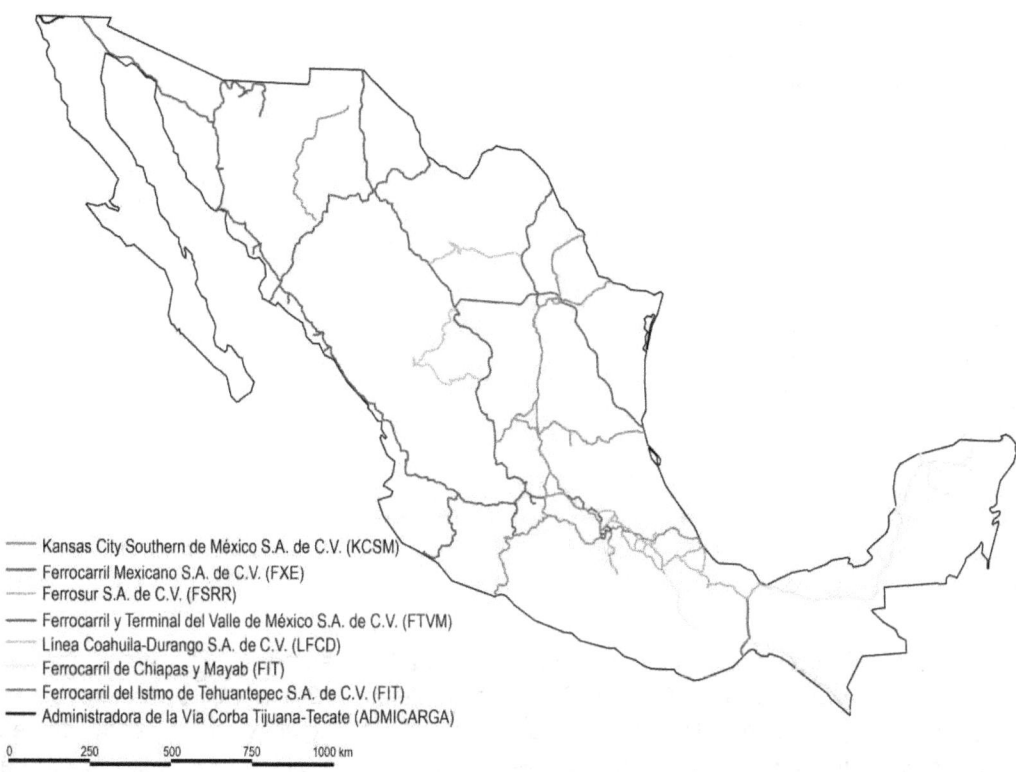

Source: ARTF (2018[12]), *Anuario Estadístico Ferroviario 2017* (Railway Statistical Yearbook 2017), https://www.gob.mx/artf/acciones-y-programas/anuario-estadistico-ferroviario-2017-152797 (accessed 31 January 2018).

Exclusivity

The main concessions were awarded for 50 years. The Law on the Regulation of Rail Services provides for concessions to be awarded for a maximum of 50 years with an option of renewal in one or more stages for a maximum of a further 50 years in total. Exclusivity to run trains over the networks in concession was granted in the concession agreements for the three trunk railways for periods of 30 years, to protect the value of the concessions and safeguard the incentive to invest in infrastructure. The smaller concessions were granted for periods of 30 years, with exclusive rights for 18 years, see Table 3.2.

Table 3.2. Concession periods for freight rail transportation in Mexico

Concession	Year awarded	Concession holders	Length (years)	Extended to (years)	Exclusivity (years)	Exclusivity extended to (years)	Current exclusive period	Current concession end
Mexico's Valley	1996	FTVM	50		50		To 2046	2046
Northeast	1996	TFM; KCSM	50		30		To 2026	2046
North-Pacific	1997	Grupo Mexico, Ferromex	50	55.5	30	35.5	To 2033	2056
Ojinaga-	1997	Grupo Mexico,	50		30		To 2033	2056

Concession	Year awarded	Concession holders	Length (years)	Extended to (years)	Exclusivity (years)	Exclusivity extended to (years)	Current exclusive period	Current concession end
Topolobampo shortline		Ferromex						
Durango-Coahuila	1997	Industriales Peñoles	30		18		To 2015	2027
Southeast	1998	Ferrosur; Grupo Mexico, Ferrosur	50		30		To 2028	2048
Nacozari shortline	1999	Grupo Mexico, Ferromex	30					2029
Chiapas-Mayab	1999	Genesee & Wyoming	30		18			
		Viabilis		50		30	To 2029	2049
		State					To be retendered	
Isthmus of Tehuantepec	1999	State	50		-			2049
Tijuana-Tecate	1999	Estado de Baja California	50		30		2029	2049
Cuautitlan-Buenavista passenger service	2005	Ferrocarriles Suburbanos	30					2035
Oaxaca and South shortline	2006	Ferrosur; State	30		30		To 2036	2036

Source: SCT (2015[11])*Anuario Estadístico Sector Comunicaciones y Transportes 2014* (2014 Statistical Yearbook of the Communications and Transport Sector), http://www.sct.gob.mx/fileadmin/DireccionesGrales/DGP/estadistica/Anuarios/Anuario_2014.pdf (accessed 3 March 2019).

Ferromex's North-Pacific concession was extended five and a half years in 2017 in return for refinancing a 25 km rail by-pass around the city of Celaya (Gobierno de Mexico, 2017[14]). By-passes on the Ferromex and KCSM lines passing through Celaya, to avoid central parts of the town, were part of the Government's national infrastructure investment plan for the five years 2014-2018. The investments were to be funded publicly. However, after construction had begun on the bypass on the North-Pacific concession line, a sharp fall in oil prices severely constrained public finances, leading the government to seek an alternate financing arrangement with Ferromex. Exclusive rights to the network in concession were similarly extended by five years and six months, to a total of 33.5 years.

Trackage and haulage rights mandated as exceptions to exclusivity

Specific trackage and haulage rights were provided for in the annexes to the concession agreements as an exception to the exclusivity granted to the concession holder. These trackage rights enable another concession holder to operate freight services over the tracks of the concession. Provisions for trackage rights were made as follows:

- Mandatory trackage rights were designated in the concession agreements for specific concession holders to be able to negotiate access arrangements, mostly by location, product and slot, with the incumbent concession on a voluntary basis. The sections of track concerned are identified more or less symmetrically in the corresponding concession agreements, with Annex 9 setting out the obligations of the concession to provide trackage rights to others and Annex 10 setting out the rights the concession holder can expect to enjoy on other parts of the national network (see Table 3.3, Table 3.4 and Table 3.5).
- The Coahuila-Durango Railway was granted trackage rights, for specific products and slots, to operate trains over a section of the Ferromex mainline to link the two parts of its concession.

- In the South, the Chiapas-Mayab concession included general trackage rights to link its two lines using the Ferrosur line between the Gulf port of Coatzacoalcos and Medias Aguas and the Isthmus railway line between Medias Aguas and the Pacific ports of Salina Cruz. Then, Ferrosur was granted general trackage rights to run its trains over the Isthmus railway line to reach the port of Salina Cruz.

The government reserved the right in the concession agreements to assign additional trackage rights for passenger trains. It also reserved to assign additional trackage and haulage rights for freight trains in the public interest – conditioned on to the economically and technically feasibility from the point of view of the concession, the international traffic and on the basis of reciprocity. Now, no test of economic feasibility has been specified neither awards on trackage or haulage rights have been made. These provisions are set out in Article 1.4.2 of the concession agreements.

The general trackage rights applied to the Isthmus railway and Ferrosur in the south have been used regularly since award of the concessions. The Coahuila-Durango railway makes regular use of its rights to Ferromex track but finds these overly restrictive. Other trackage and haulage rights has proved to be problematic, nonetheless they are regularly used, as exemplified by the protracted negotiations between KCSM and Ferromex outlined in the previous section.

The exclusive right to carry freight has now lapsed on one concession, ending in 2015 for the Coahuila-Durango railway. There has been no entry by another concession into markets served by this railway.

Table 3.3. Mandatory trackage rights assigned and received in concession titles in Mexico

Concession holder	Trackage rights assigned (km)	Trackage rights received (km)	Number of trackage rights received	Trackage rights assigned plus received (km)
Grupo Mexico	8 643	1 611	36	10 254
Ferromex	7 164	1 035	24	8 199
Ferrosur	1 479	575	12	2 054
KCSM	4 283	1 602	30	5 885
FIT	219	n.a.	1	219
Chiapas Mayab	1 550	n.a.	10	1 155
Coahuila Durango	974	304	2	1 278
FERROVALLE	297	45	1	342

Source: COFECE (2016[4]), *Reporte Preliminar sobre Competencia Efectiva en el Sistema Ferroviario Mexicano* (Preliminary report on the Effective Competition in the Mexican Railway System).

Table 3.4. Mandatory trackage and haulage rights included in the concession titles in Mexico

Concession	Obligations to other concession holders (number of trackage rights)	Rights to other concessioned networks (number of trackage rights)
Northeast railway line, under concession to KCSM	11 Ferromex 6 Ferrosur 2 Hidalgo railway line (Ferrosur) 1 FERROVALLE	11 North-Pacific Railway Line (Ferromex) 3 Southeast Railway Line (Ferrosur) 3 South Railway Line (Ferrosur) 1 Mexico's valley Railway Line (FERROVALLE)
Pacific-North Railway Line, under concession to Ferromex	7 KCSM 2 Coahuila-Durango 2 Nacozari Railway Line (Ferromex)	11 Northeast Railway Line (KCSM) 1 Mexico's valley Railway Line (FERROVALLE) 1 Coahuila-Durango Railway Line
Nacozari Railway Line, under concession to Ferromex	2 Railway Line North-Pacific (Ferromex)	2 Pacific North Railway Line (Ferromex)

Concession	Obligations to other concession holders (number of trackage rights)	Rights to other concessioned networks (number of trackage rights)
Ojinaga Topolobampo Railway Line, under concession to Ferromex	1 Railway Line North-Pacific (Ferromex)	4 Railway Line North-Pacific (Ferromex)
Southeast Railway Line, under concession to Ferrosur	2 KCSM 4 Chiapas and Mayab 2 Oaxaca and South 1 Via Corta Tres Valles-San Cristobal (Ferrosur)	4 Northeast Railway Line (KCSM) 6 Mexico's Valley Railway Line (FERROVALLE) 1 Via Corta Isthmus of Tehuantepec (FIT) 1 Via Corta del Sur (Ferrosur)
Mexico Valley Railway Line, under concession to FERROVALLE	7 KCSM 1 Ferromex 4 Southeast Railway Line (Ferrosur) 1 Via Corta del Sur (Ferrosur)	1 Northeast Railway Line (KCSM)
Coahuila-Durango Railway Line	1 Ferromex (for unit trains of fuel between Torreon and Villa Juarez)	2 Pacific-North Railway Line (Ferromex)
Chiapas and Mayab Railway Lines	None	Chiapas: 1 Southeast Railway Line (Ferrosur); 5 Isthmus of Tehuantepec Railway Line Chiapas y Mayab: 1 Southeast Railway Line
Isthmus of Tehuantepec Railway Line	1 Ferrosur 6 Chiapas and Mayab	1 Southeast Railway Line (Ferrosur) between Medias Aguas and Coatzocoalcos
South and Oaxaca Railway Lines	1 Southeast Railway Line (Ferrosur) 1 KCSM (for unit and wagonload trains)	2 Southeast Railway Line (Ferrosur) 1 Northeast Railway Line (KCSM)

Source: COFECE (2016[4]), *Reporte Preliminar sobre Competencia Efectiva en el Sistema Ferroviario Mexicano* (Preliminary report on the Effective Competition in the Mexican Railway System).

Captive shipper protection

To protect captive shippers, where COFECE determines an absence of effective competition, the Law on the Regulation of Rail Services (Article 47) provided for shippers to request the imposition of regulated tariffs or for the regulator to take the initiative to impose such tariffs.

The concession titles provide for trackage and haulage rights to be awarded anywhere on the rail network on request by users, or potential users, where absence of effective competition is determined by COFECE. This is the subject of Article 3 of the concession titles and detailed in Annex 9 of each concession. These rights can substitute for the regulated tariffs provided for in the Law. Such trackage and haulage rights are specific to the trip and products for which there are deemed to be no viable alternatives and apply to a specific origin and destination so that intermediate points cannot be served. They can be assigned on the tracks of a concession only after a period of 20 years has elapsed since award of the concession and come into force one year after the decision to grant trackage or haulage rights.

The protection for captive shippers provided by this concession title clause is an alternative to the general power of the regulator to impose tariffs in situations where there is no effective competition, to which the 20-year exemption period does not apply. COFECE (2016[4]) interprets the 20-year period of exemption from the exercise of these trackage and haulage rights as exempting concessions from the application of regulated tariffs under Article 47 of the Law on the Regulation of Rail Services, which would appear counter to the intention of the Law. Regardless of the orientation of these views, the ARTF will face an increase in the demand of its functions and resources as the 20-year period of exclusivity will expire relatively soon for most concessions (see Table 3.2).

Table 3.5. Example of trackage and haulage rights in concession titles in Mexico: North-Pacific Concession

Rights (Valid from initiation of concession for its duration, unless specified otherwise)	Valid from	Period of validity	Used from (to)
Obligations imposed in Annex 9 of the concession on the holder to provide rights to other train operators:			
Trackage rights for the Railway Line Northeast			
Mariscala-Guadalajara for wagon load trains with origin/destination in the industrial zone of Guadalajara, with the objective of increasing rail-on-rail competition.	12 months after award of concession	To end of concession	
Pedro Morales-Cerro La Silla for wagon load trains, mainly carrying fuels.			
Topo Grande-Chipinque for movements between the Monterrey platform and Chipinque to form trains using the line to Torreon.			
Celaya-Silao for unit trains for the auto industry to serve General Motors.			
Arbol Grande-Altamira to provide access to Ciudad Madero, Altamira and Miramar (in the Tampico conurbation on the Gulf Coast).			
Arellano-Chicalote to serve Nissan in Arellano with unit trains and enable exchange of wagons in Aguascalientes.			
Viborillas-Huehuetoca for operation of double stack trains and/or multi-level automobile trains to heights allowed by the catenaries on the double track line between Mexico City and Queretaro.	Initiation of Northeast concession	2 years	
Trackage rights for the Railway Line Nacozari			
On sections of the Nogales line for trains requiring interchange with the North-Pacific Railway (Ferromex) in Nogales or at the frontier with the Union Pacific Southern Pacific Railroad.			
Nogales-Guaymas for unit trains of sulfuric acid or minerals for export.			
Trackage rights for the Railway Line Coahuila-Durango			
Sabinas-Ciudad Frontera for unit trains carrying coal and coke between Barroteran and Sabinas.			
Torreon-Escalon for unit trains carrying iron ore.			
Trackage rights for the Railway Line Ojinaga-Topolobampo			
Tabaloapa-Chihuahua to provide access to the shunting yard and intermodal terminal of the North-Pacific railway (Ferromex)			
Chihuahua-Ciudad Juarez, railhead of the Burlington Northern Sante Fe Railroad and link to railhead of the Union Pacific Southern Pacific Railroad for exchange of wagons with US railroads.			
Sufragio yard for trains needing to use the weigh station in the yard, until installation of a weight station on the Railway Line Ojinaga-Topolobampo.	Inititation of Ojinaga-Topolobampo concession	One year.	
Trackage and haulage rights on the whole network			
On request by users or potential users where absence of effective competition is determined under Article 47 of the Law on the Regulation of Rail Services. These rights can substitute for the regulated tariffs provided for in the Law. Such rights are specific to the trip and products for which there are deemed to be no viable alternatives and apply to a specific origin and destination so that intermediate points cannot be served.	20 years after award of the concession. And one year after rights awarded.	To end of concession	None
Awarded by the government, SCT (now ARTF).	5 years after rights awarded.	To end of concession	
Rights awarded in Annex 10 of the concession to the holder to exercise rights on the lines of other train operators:			
Railway Line Northeast			
Viborillas-Encantada for wagon load trains to use line B to connect with traffic in Queretaro and Mexico City (in conjunction with following trackage right).	12 months after award of Northeast concession	To end of concession	
Ramos Arzipe-Encantada for unit trains with origin/destination in Rojas,			

Rights (Valid from initiation of concession for its duration, unless specified otherwise)	Valid from	Period of validity	Used from (to)
Saltillo or Encantada to use lines B and BS.			
Topo Grande-Monterrey freight yard-Cerro La Silla to provide access to the Monterrey yard and connection to lines to Torreon and Tampico.			
Apodaca-Matamoros to serve the industrial zone of Lagrange and Apodaca with wagonload trains.			
Monterrey Freight Yard-Leona to serve the industrial zone of Leona with wagon load trains,			
Tampico-Arbol Grande-Doña Cecilia for wagon load trains with origin or destination in Tampico or Doña Cecilia.			
La Griega-Mariscala on double electrified Juarez and Morelos lines for all trains. For Hecules to Mariscala section duration for 3 years only.			
Celaya-Escobedo for access to the Escobedo interchange yard.			
Buenavista-Huehuetoca for trains with origin or destination in Buenavista, Pantaco, Mexico Valley Terminal and Lecheria.			
San Juan del Rio-San Nicolas for wagon load trains for access to the industrial zone of San Juan del Rio			
La Griega-Huehuetoca for use of the electrified double track line in case of congestion on Line B.	Initiation of the Northeast concession	2 years	
Railway Line del Valle de Mexico			
4 sections of line for traffic with origin or destination in Pantaco, Valle de Mexico and Lecheria that needs to use lines A or B.			
Railway Line Coahuila-Durango			
Torreon-Villa Juarez for unit trains carrying fuels.			
Trackage and haulage rights on the whole network			
Trackage and haulage rights on request to SCT (now ARTF) in conformity with the Law on the Regulation of Rail Services and where no other limitation to the award of such rights prevails.	Date of award	To end of concession	None

Source: Annexes to North-Pacific concession Gobierno de México (1997[15]), *Concesión otorgada en favor de Ferrocarril Pacífico-Norte, S.A. de C.V., respecto de la Vía corta Ojinaga-Topolobampo* [Concession granted in favor of Ferrocarril Pacífico-Norte, S.A. de C.V., with respect to the Short Vía Ojinaga-Topolobampo], http://www.dof.gob.mx/nota_detalle.php?codigo=4903433&fecha=11/12/1997CONCESION otorgada en favor de Ferrocarril Pacífico-Norte, S.A. de C.V., respecto de la Vía corta Ojinaga-Topolobampo publicly available in different format in COFECE (2016[4]), *Reporte Preliminar sobre Competencia Efectiva en el Sistema Ferroviario Mexicano* (Preliminary report on the Effective Competition in the Mexican Railway System).

Trackage rights negotiated in addition to those mandated in concession titles

Since award of the concessions a number of additional trackage rights have been agreed between concession holders by mutual consent. Ferromex has granted KCSM some trackage rights that extend those included in the concession titles to adjoining areas in four instances. KSM has granted very limited privileges of a similar nature to Ferromex in two cases and rights that help decongest lines in a metropolitan area in one case. Ferrosur granted Chiapas-Mayab rights to use 420 km of its tracks (COFECE, 2016[4]).

2015 Amendments to the Law and Establishment of the Regulatory Agency for Rail Transport

Network objectives

The 1995 railway reforms achieved a complete turnaround in the performance of the Mexican railway sector (ITF, 2014[16]). Profitable concessions replaced a State-run railway that operated at a large and growing deficit. The concession holders invested in rolling stock and infrastructure, greatly improving freight services and facilitating economic growth and in particular a large volume of inward investment in the auto industry.

Nevertheless, the incomplete use of the trackage and haulage rights provided for in the concession agreements may indicate an unexploited potential for further improvements in efficiency and quality of service. Article 35 of the 1995 law provides for interconnecting services between the concessions through the use of these rights and there was criticism that the system was not working as intended as a national network. Dissatisfaction was exacerbated by the failure of concessions to agree on terms for the use of some of the most prominent mandated trackage rights in the concession agreements and subsequent rejection in court of the conditions imposed by SCT for use of these rights. Some shippers also saw the capacity of the authorities to implement the protection from abusive tariffs provided by Article 47 of the law as inadequate. At the same time, proposals to cease operation of some unprofitable freight lines, for example through Oaxaca City was rejected by the government as counter to national development objectives and the ending of passenger services on all but three lines was regretted by the public and seen by commentators less familiar with rail markets as a sign of failure.

This led to a series of amendments to the 1995 law being proposed in 2013 by legislators in the Chamber of Deputies. Reinforcement of arrangements for use of trackage rights was proposed together with additional rights of access to the networks in concession. Had all of the proposals been adopted, the resulting erosion of exclusivity might have seen the value of the concessions significantly reduced, putting at risk further investment by the major concession holders. Following discussion in the Senate in 2014, the proposals for additional access rights were dropped, retaining amendments to reinforce existing clauses in the law and adding proposals to enhance the capacity of the government for implementing trackage rights and tariff protection through establishment of the Regulatory Agency for Rail Transport (ARTF). These amendments were adopted and the law modified in 2015. There were further modifications to the law, adopted in 2016 and 2018, that added precision on procedures for reporting regulatory information to the Agency.

The 2015 amendments make some significant additions to the objectives of the law, set out in Article 1, adding guarantee of interconnection between rail lines, establishment of conditions for competition in rail services and operational efficiency. Whilst interconnection and competition can improve operational efficiency, they can also be difficult to reconcile with recovery of the costs of investment in infrastructure. The most important duty of the ARTF is to find the most effective balance between these objectives in fostering the long-term development of sustainable, high quality rail services. Striking this balance is a challenge in all jurisdictions and the reason that specialised rail regulators have been established in many countries in addition to competition authorities. Whilst the importance of viewing the rail system as a national network and fostering interconnecting services across the concessions is now clearly indicated in the Law, efficiency and preserving incentives for private investment from the concessions remain essential.

Tariffs and competition

The large fixed costs and relatively low marginal costs of rail transport mean that the most efficient use of the system is made when freight is charged in inverse relation to its price elasticity. That is, freight that cannot easily transfer to road or waterborne transport is charged as much as it can bear whilst still being competitive in the market, whilst freight that can easily switch is charged closer to the marginal cost of transport. Differentiating charges in this way to recover costs and provide for reasonable profit maximises the value of the rail service for society overall. This result was demonstrated a century ago by economist Frank Ramsey and developed into the basis for regulating the prices charged by natural monopolies 30 years later by Marcel Boiteux (Ramsey, 1927[17]) (Boiteux, 1956[18]). It provides the basis for the regulation of rail tariffs in Mexico and the rest of North America and many other countries.

Arguably, a single network-wide rail operator might be most efficient, but large markets can support competition in rail services, and competition is the most effective way of moderating prices and improving services. This is built into the structure of the Mexican concessions, where two concessions serve each of the largest markets and in the valley of Mexico the jointly owned concession provides equal access to three concessions. In the USA, the Surface Transportation Board under pressure from the Department of Justice introduced a moratorium on mergers between US Class 1 Railways in 2000 to preserve this kind of rail-on-rail competition issuing rules in 2001. The moratorium put the onus of proof on merger applicants that the effect of a merger would be procompetitive rather than anticompetitive (Pittman, 2017[19]). Over the rest of the Mexican network, the exclusive right to provide rail services enables the railways to apply Ramsey-Boiteux pricing and cover costs efficiently.

In most of Europe, in contrast, the railways charge freight prices close to marginal cost, and open access provisions in conformity with European Union law promote more atomistic competition to carry freight. This is possible because freight transport contributes little or nothing to fixed costs in most of Europe (see Table 3.6 for an example from the UK). Passenger trains are the prime user of most of Europe's rail networks; they have priority over freight which is often relegated to off-peak slots and secondary lines. Passenger traffic covers fixed costs, to a greater or lesser extent, with a large part of infrastructure costs covered by government budgets. In principle, no freight is carried below marginal cost but charging full wear and tear costs to heavy trains, carrying steel for example, has proved politically controversial at times. When the Betuwe freight line serving Rotterdam was opened in 2007 for example, the Minister of Transport intervened to reduce prices for the heaviest cargos below marginal costs and was obliged by the regulator to provide compensation to the infrastructure manager for the loss of revenue. A national General Audit Office reports that between 2006 and 2013 EUR 17 million was spent by the Ministry to compensate for lower tariffs and tariff incentives (Algemene Rekenkamer, 2016[20]).

The UK Office of Rail Regulation (now Office of Rail and Road, ORR) reviewed opportunities to charge a mark-up over marginal cost on the carriage of coal and other heavy freight in 2006. The objective was to help cover fixed costs by charging more in markets that had been growing. However, the ORR found the markets too fragile to sustain such charges and concluded that the operator would be better at determining demand elasticities than the regulator. The contribution of freight to the total revenue of Network Rail, the infrastructure operator in the UK, is only around 0.5%, see Table 3.6. Preliminary results from the ORR's latest five-year Periodic Review of Network Rail's business plans, released in June 2018, confirm the freight contribution will not increase. ORR proposes that the variable network access charges for freight are capped, so that they only increase to reflect the full costs of wear-and-tear on the network (as required by legislation) towards the end of the control period, which runs from 2024 to 2029 (ORR, 2018[21]).

Table 3.6. Network Rail Income in England and Wales

2011- 2012

Source	Income, 2011-2012 prices (GBP Billions)	Share (%)
Passengers	7.2	58
Commercial operations such as shops and car parks	1.3	10
Subsidy from the taxpayer	4.0	32
Freight	0.064	0.5
Total	12.5	100

Source: ORR (2013[22]), *Periodic Review 2013*, http://orr.gov.uk/rail/economic-regulation/regulation-of-network-rail/price-controls/periodic-review-2013/pr13-guide/about-pr13. (accessed 10 March 2019).

Where freight rail services have to cover the full cost of the network, as in Mexico, Canada, and the US, Ramsey-Boiteux pricing is the starting point for efficient charges. Regulators may need to intervene to protect captive shippers and to promote interconnection, but this should be done on a case-by-case basis as there is no simple alternative pricing formula that can be applied across the network.

Responsibilities for economic regulation

The amended Law on the Regulation of Rail Services assigns specific duties to ARTF in the Article 6 Bis. ARTF is charged with guaranteeing interconnection and, when concessions are unable to reach agreement on trackage or haulage rights, establishing conditions of access and charges for interconnection. ARTF is also charged with collecting the information and developing the tools to be in a position to exercise this authority.

Article 36 of the law requires concession holders to provide other concessions holders with interconnection services and associated trackage or haulage rights in return for fair compensation. The ARTF is charged with establishing access rights and charges where these are not agreed voluntarily.

Article 36 of the law provides for the Agency to establish mandatory trackage rights on specific routes when COFECE finds an absence of effective competition in a specific area. These rights will be for specific products and specific points of origin and destination. The conditions imposed must take into account principles recognised internationally and the Agency can consult with COFECE in making its determination.

Article 36 also gives shippers the right to choose, when transport over the lines of two concessions is involved, between paying tariffs set independently by the two concession holders for each part of the route or a tariff set for the whole route by one or other of the concession holders. The law omits to specify what action a shipper might take if neither concession proposes a tariff or if the proposals are unacceptable, and no role is identified for the Agency (or for COFECE) in the absence of agreement. This is a gap in the legislation that should be closed.

Article 46 provides for the concessions to set tariffs freely. This is essential for financial sustainability, and freeing tariffs from controls was the single most important factor in the recovery of freight railways in the USA following the 1980 reform under the Staggers Act. Roughly half of all freight in Mexico is transported under confidential negotiated contracts. In the United States the proportion is higher.

Article 47 provides protection from abusive tariffs for captive shippers, requiring the Agency to establish of its own accord or at the request of an affected party, the basis for regulated tariffs in cases where COFECE identifies an absence of effective competition.

In July 2018, the Agency issued a proposal on tariffs for captive shippers for comment by stakeholders. The basis for tariffs eventually agreed under this proposal could also provide the basis for access charges under Articles 35 and 36 of the law. This will fill a gap in tools for implementing the access rights provided for in the law.

At the same time, the primacy given to voluntary agreement by the law, the limited circumstances in which the Agency can intervene and the procedure to be followed to identify specific circumstances in which (rail and road) competition is insufficient, protect the concessions from undue interference in their freedom to set prices.

Additional amendments to the Law on the Regulation of Rail Services

In June 2016 the Article 8 Bis was added to the Law on the Regulation of Rail Services. It states that for granting new concession titles or extensions, the Ministry of Communications and Transport must deliver to the Ministry of Finance a report with the economic profitability of the project, along with the supporting documents. The document must include the regulatory contribution that must be paid by the concessionaire. The Ministry of Finance will have 30 calendar days to approve or reject it. Also, the project would have to be registered in the list of programmes and investment projects of the Ministry of Finance when it considers public investment as part of the project's funding.

The 2018's amendments of the law include modifications to the Article 46 regarding the tariff's section. Now, all the modifications to maximum tariffs will have to be registered previously with the ARTF detailing the service that will be provided for each, excepting those agreed between concessionaires and users. These must be available at any time for the Agency. The concessionaires will have to register with the Agency, the list of services and charges and its application rules.

In order to modify the maximum tariff, the concessionaire will have to justify it, and the Agency will be able to give recommendations about it. When the Agency considers convenient, it can ask for COFECE's opinion in terms of competition.

International practice on regulation and governance of the rail sector

International practice in setting principles for regulated tariffs and trackage rights is relevant, and stipulated in the Law to Regulate Rail Services as a factor to be taken into account by ARTF in making regulatory decisions. Given the structure of the railways in Mexico and the dominance of freight transport, the USA and Canada are the most relevant jurisdictions for comparison. There are, however, two significant differences between Mexico and the other railway systems of North America. First US and Canadian railways have no contracts with the government to define the specific rights of the railroads and the regulators can implement regulatory remedies independently of any such considerations. Mexican regulation will have to strike a balance between enforcing contract rights and obligations and the ability to regulate behaviour on other grounds. Second, the modal split in freight transport is much more heavily weighted toward trucks in Mexico than in the US or Canada, see Figure 3.4. Most Mexican concessions face more truck competition than US or Canadian railways, narrowing the range of situations in which there is likely to be no effective competition. The mix of commodities in Mexico is much more susceptible to truck competition than in the US or Canada, see Figure 3.5. The starting point for regulation is inherently different in Mexico because the underlying presumption of effective competition, valid already in most markets in the USA, will be even more prevalent in Mexico.

Figure 3.4. International comparisons of rail share of rail vs truck ton-km (%)

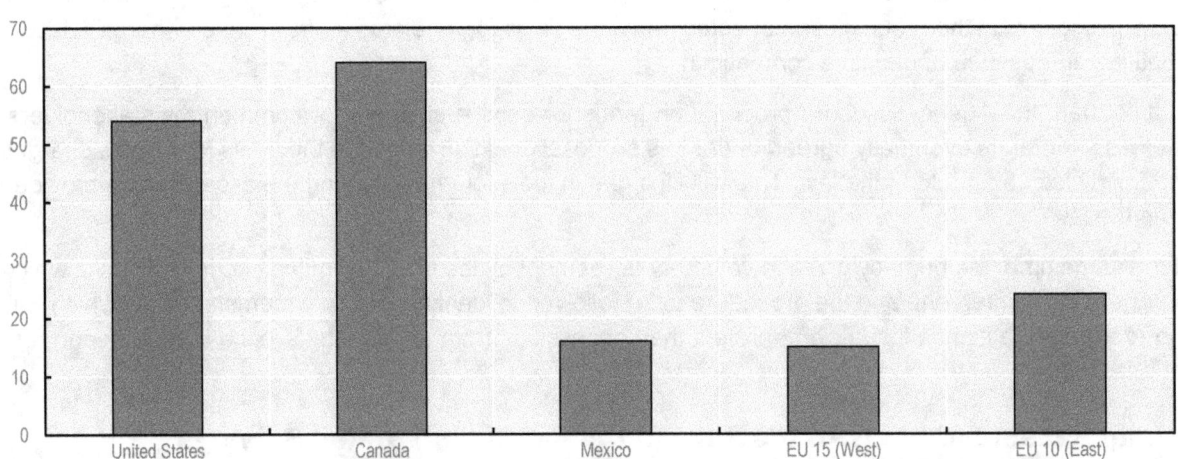

Source: AAR (2019[23]), *Rail Traffic Data*, Association of American Railroads, https://www.aar.org/data-center/rail-traffic-data/ (accessed 5 March 2019); RAC (2013[24]), *2014 Rail Trends*, https://www.railcan.ca/wp-content/uploads/2016/10/2014_RAC_RailTrends.pdf (accessed 5 March 2019); SCT (2015[11]) *Anuario Estadístico Sector Comunicaciones y Transportes 2014* [2014 Statistical Yearbook of the Communications and Transport Sector], http://www.sct.gob.mx/fileadmin/DireccionesGrales/DGP/estadistica/Anuarios/Anuario_2014.pdf. (accessed 3 March 2019). ITF (2018[25]), *ITF Transport Statistics-Goods Transport*, http://dx.doi.org/10.1787/trsprt-data-en.

Figure 3.5. Rail commodity distribution in North America

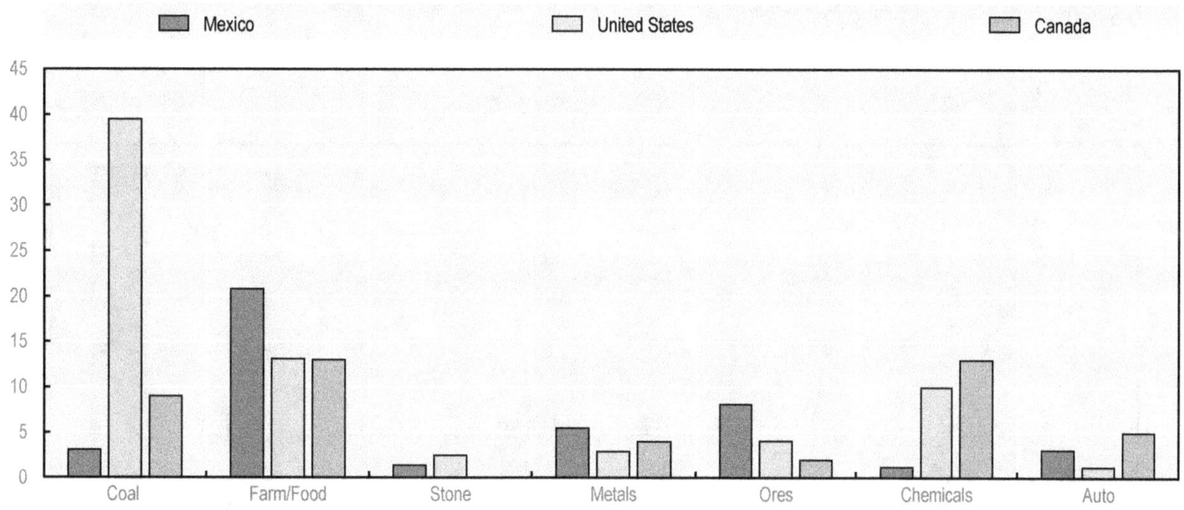

Note: Mexico and the United States are indicated in % of tones and Canada in % of carloads.
Source: STB (2018[26]), *Statistics of Class 1 Freight Railroads*, https://www.stb.gov/Econdata.nsf/M%20Statistics%20of%20Class%201%20Feight%20RR?OpenPage (accessed 5 March 2019); RAC (2013[24]), *2014 Rail Trends*, https://www.railcan.ca/wp-content/uploads/2016/10/2014_RAC_RailTrends.pdf (accessed 5 March 2019); SCT (2014[27]), *Anuario Estadístico, Sector Comunicaciones y Transporte 2013* [2013 Statistical Yearbook, Communications and Transport Sector], http://www.sct.gob.mx/fileadmin/DireccionesGrales/DGP/estadistica/Anuarios/Anuario-2013.pdf.

The US and Canadian regulation reflects the implications of relatively high fixed costs and low marginal costs in providing rail services. If railways are to recover their fixed costs they must be able to charge tariffs that, in total, depart sufficiently from marginal costs to generate the difference between marginal and fixed costs. This has resulted in a Ramsey pricing approach to rail tariffs in the US and Canada, which means that every shipper pays prices that are as far above marginal costs as its price elasticity of demand permits, limited by the potential for regulators to intervene to prevent abuse of market power and undue discrimination for non-market reasons. The US approach has led to a wide range of average tariffs by commodity and of ratios of revenue to variable cost (see Figure 3.6). Note however, that the methodology used by the US regulator for measuring variable costs has been subject to intense criticism, see, for example, (McCullough, 2008[28]) and (Huneke, 2017[29]).

Figure 3.6 makes clear that there is a wide range of prices (revenue/tonne-km) and ratios of coverage of fixed costs in the overall US rail system today. Food, for example, travels at an average ratio of 168%, well below the 180% that, on average, would reflect full coverage of fixed costs. If food were raised to 180%, some traffic would have to be charged more, raising prices to the consumer of food, and some would either not move or would be forced to shift to trucks, again raising prices. Chemicals, by contrast, move at a ratio of 234%. Of course, the chemical industry would like to pay less, but the fact is the prices charged do not price traffic off the market or make the chemical industry uncompetitive, and the pricing ensures that, among other things, the food traffic can move at 168% without wrecking the finances of the railways. Note that Figure 3.6 is based on masked revenues that, on average, are about 25% higher than actual revenues, though the excess percentage varies between 10% and 50% depending on commodity. The basic import of the figure is the wide range of prices and the variation in coverage ratios remains.

Figure 3.6. U.S. freight railway tariff structure with revenue masked

2016 US cents/tonne-km and ratio in percentage

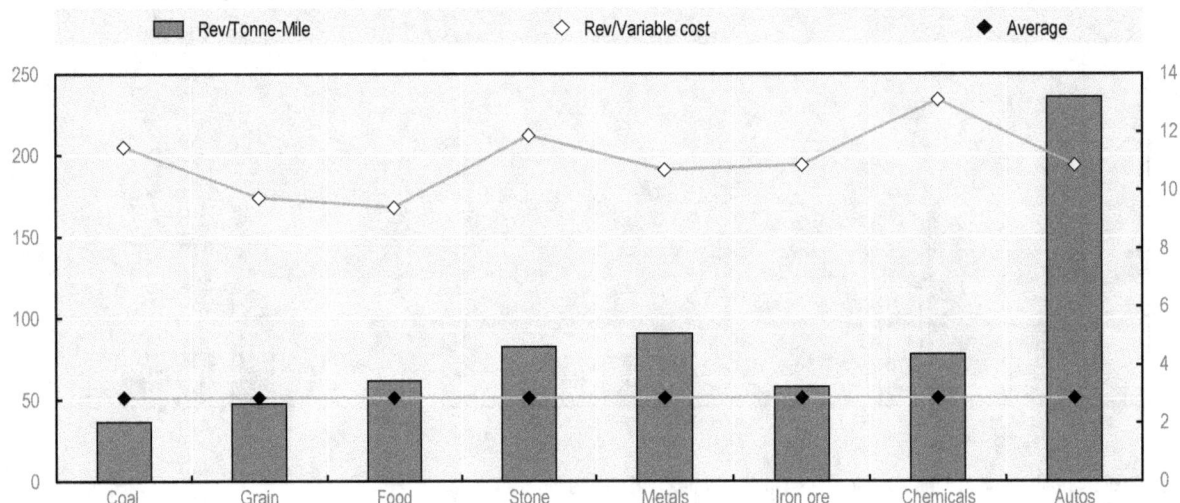

Source: STB (2019[30]), *Carload Waybill Sample* (2 digit STCC level), https://www.stb.gov/stb/industry/econ_waybill.html (accessed 6 March 2019).

US methodologies

The US and Canadian governments have adopted an approach to regulation that accepts the tenets of Ramsey pricing and focuses on attempting to limit abuse of market power in circumstances where market power exists – in the United States, or in providing regulatory tools to shippers such as final offer arbitration, inter-switching, level of service complaints (in Canada) to balance the relationships between shippers and railways.

In the US, this is done principally by regulating specific rates where there is found to be abuse of a particular captive shipper– defined as a shipper lacking economic alternatives, intra-modal or inter-modal, to the serving railroad. In other words railways are allowed and indeed expected to adjust their prices (discriminate or engage in differential pricing) among shippers in the tariffs applied, including for transport of the same commodities, in order to be able to cover costs and operate at a profit overall.

The US approach to rail regulation originated in 1887 with the creation of the Interstate Commerce Commission (ICC). Based on populist reaction to abuses by the "Rail Barons" in the mid-1800s rail prices and charging practices were controlled in many ways that were intended to rein in the railroad owners, protect other modes, protect certain shippers or classes of shippers, and to force railroads to absorb social burdens within their commercial activities. US regulation expanded over the years to cover trucks and barges and attempted, mostly without success, to adjust to the new competitive conditions that emerged after World War II. As a result, by the 1970s, the entire US railroad system was in poor financial condition.

The government took two steps to change the situation: first, Amtrak was created in 1971 to shift the burden of passenger losses onto Federal and state hands; and, second, US railways were substantially deregulated through the 1980 Staggers Act (trucking and airlines were deregulated at nearly the same time) in order to allow transportation markets to respond to market forces. The US Congress further reinforced this trend toward deregulation in 1995 when it abolished the old ICC and created a new regulator, the Surface Transportation Board (STB), with a narrower scope of regulation to enforce.

In addition to easing abandonments and allowing more flexibility in tariff-setting, the STB totally exempted from regulation all rail tariffs for voluntary contracts between shippers and railroads. Voluntary contracts often include conditions on investment by railway and shipper, service quality commitments, minimum volumes to be shipped and ancillary services such as packaging and warehousing that reflect a complex balance of interests for which regulation is unnecessary, clumsy, and/or inappropriate. A number of specific commodities or groups of commodities (most agricultural products) and some types of services (intermodal and boxcar) have also been exempted because highway and/or barge competition is presumed to be a powerful restraint on rail pricing. The extensive use of exemptions is in part motivated by the concern that regulation often does more harm than good, as many years of overregulation clearly showed.

The STB does not usually prescribe competitive access. The philosophy of the Staggers Act was that adequate competition should be presumed to exist and that regulation should be used only to correct cases of abuse of market power. Overall, the STB estimates that only 10% of all US railroad freight traffic is subject to any form of regulation (Huneke, 2017[29]). Rates and service on the other 90% of the traffic are assumed to be constrained by competition, which may come from motor or water carriers (intermodal competition) for some commodities or from other railroads (intramodal competition) for other commodities. Regarding both intermodal and intramodal competition, both parallel competition (two carriers serving the same origin-destination pair) and geographic competition (two carriers both serving the same origin and/or both serving the same destination) have been shown to be effective in protecting shippers from anticompetitive behaviour by railroads (Mac Donald, 1989[31]) and (Mac Donald, 1987[32]).

Rates for non-exempt commodities and services that might potentially be regulated are subject to a regulatory regime that has been called constrained market pricing (CMP), which is intended to strike a balance between market forces and the potential for abuse of market power where it exists (ICC, 1985[33]) and (STB, 2006[34])

Two baseline conditions must be met before the STB may regulate the tariffs charged by a railroad to a shipper:

- There is shown to be an absence of effective competition from other railroads or from trucks or barges.
- The tariff for the traffic in question has an existing or proposed ratio of revenue to variable cost that is greater than 180%.

If these two conditions are met, shippers may request rate protection from the STB based on one of three grounds:

- The railroad company is managed inefficiently, and shippers should not be forced to pay the price for this;
- The railroad company is earning "economic profits", and shippers should not be forced to contribute to these;
- The rate charged exceeds the "stand-alone cost" of serving the shipper, where this means the theoretical cost of creating an entirely separate railway to serve just the shipper's traffic.

In practice, up to now STB rate cases have been brought almost exclusively under the stand-alone-cost provision of the regulations. The stand-alone-cost test is designed to assess for the presence of cross-subsidisation. Though controversial, it is a standard component of some regulatory regimes for some infrastructure sectors around the world, perhaps most widely used in the postal sector. It is based on (Faulhaber, 1975[35]), and further discussion is available in (Baumol, 1987[36]), (ACCC, 2014[37]) and (Decker, 2018[38]).

The STB normally does not act on its own volition, but rather acts when a shipper complains. Much of US regulation ultimately relies on adversarial proceedings with the STB deciding after hearing argument from all parties. STB proceedings are open to all, and any party wishing to be heard can ask to appear or can file material it considers relevant. Although the focus is necessarily on the questions relevant to constrained market pricing and in particular the stand-alone-cost test, all other potentially relevant issues can be raised and considered.

STB decisions can be appealed if they can be shown to violate agency procedures or other federal law, but the agency's findings of fact are generally accepted by courts as correct. There is a presumption in the courts that the agency is best qualified to make decisions based on economic judgment, as is the case with regulators and expert agencies in other sectors of the US economy–the so-called *Chevron* standard of administrative deference (*Chevron U.S.A., Inc. v. Natural Resources Defense Council, Inc.*, 467 U.S. 837, 1984). In those fairly rare cases where the rate charged has been found to be above stand-alone cost, the remedy has been an STB order for the railroad to both reduce the rate and refund the excess charges.

STB is mindful of the opportunity for discussion and mediation as a way to forestall formal regulation and provides technical support for shipper/railway discussion and mediation – if both sides request it. For this, it uses a separate team of experts from those involved in making regulatory determinations.

The old US Interstate Commerce Commission used to try to make average allocations of fixed costs based on shares of tons and ton-km, or on shares of wagonloads and wagon-km, or on shares of revenue. The Commission eventually gave up, partly because the method of calculation of variable versus fixed costs was so unreliable and partly because it became clear that the method would under-price the high-rated commodities and over-price, and drive off the railroad, the low-rated commodities (Kahn, 1971[39]).

US regulation accepts Ramsey pricing and since the 1980 Staggers Act allows railways to negotiate tariffs in confidential contracts, focusing on identifying and rectifying cases in which market power has been abused. The regulatory proceedings impose a substantial effort on the shipper to establish abuse (and on the railroad company to defend its rates). Producing stand-alone cost estimates that stand up to scrutiny at the STB and in a court appeal is expensive, requiring sometimes multimillion dollar consulting contracts (Pittman, 2010[40]). Both the usefulness of the 180% of marginal cost ratio and this application of the stand-alone-cost test have been challenged without economic foundation, including in a review by the Transportation Research Board of the National Academy of Sciences (TRB) (TRB, 2015[41]).

The TRB recommended development of a more reliable screening tool that would compare disputed rates to those charged in similarly situated competitive rail markets, saying this tool would replace current methods that make artificial and arbitrary estimates of the cost of rail shipping. The econometric studies required to benchmark performance against competitive markets would however, also require substantial effort and the recommendations have not been adopted. (Pittman, 2010[42]), (Pittman, 2010[40]) and (Pittman, 2016[43]) has argued that such a comparison would give an incentive for railroads to raise their rates in competitive markets, and has proposed a commodity-specific ceiling on tariffs or margins as a further candidate replacement mechanism (most "captive shippers" in the US ship one of only three commodities: coal, grain, or bulk chemicals.)

The STB continues to investigate potential improvements to address the shortcomings identified by the TRB, see Box 3.1. In short, the regulatory regimes currently used are not ideal, but better methods have yet to be developed.

Box 3.1. Short summary of TRB conclusions on modernising US freight rail regulation

Rate relief: more appropriate, reliable, and usable procedures are needed

While the Staggers Rail Act affords shippers the ability to challenge unusually high rates, the committee found that the formula used to identify high rates is unreliable, economically invalid, and expensive to use, thereby systematically denying large numbers of shippers the access to the law's maximum rate protections. The problem lies with the law's requirement that regulators estimate the stand-alone cost of transporting rail shipments when most railroad costs are shared by traffic and not traceable to the individual shipments under dispute. When the Staggers Rail Act was passed, all railroad pricing had been regulated, and hence there were no competitively determined rates that could serve as benchmarks for assessing the reasonableness of rates in markets with no effective competition. Three decades later, ample data on market-based rates are available for such purposes.

The study committee recommends that Congress prepare for the repeal of the current formula for screening rates for eligibility for rate relief by directing the U.S. Department of Transportation to develop a more reliable screening tool that compares disputed rates to those charged in competitive rail markets. This tool would replace current methods that make artificial and arbitrary estimates of the cost of rail shipping.

Current adjudication methods can cost millions of dollars for litigation and some have taken years to resolve, deterring shippers with smaller claims from seeking rate relief. Simplified methods that are designed to be economically valid and practical to use have been introduced but rarely utilised. In effect, the system has the effect of safeguarding railroad revenues by making it too costly for most shippers to litigate a case. Shippers are thus denied equal and effective access to the law's maximum rate protections.

The study committee recommends that STB hearings used to rule on the reasonableness of challenged rates be replaced with arbitration hearings that compel faster, more economical resolutions of rate cases. The committee also recommends that arbitrators be empowered to propose the remedy of reciprocal switching for those rates found to be unreasonable. As noted above, the committee presents a candidate test based on a comparison of the rate paid by the "captive shipper" to rates paid on comparable shipments in more competitive settings; the report includes a paper (Wilson and Wolak, 2016[44]) suggesting how this might be implemented.

Annual revenue adequacy determination serves no constructive purpose

The Staggers Rail Act requires the STB to maintain standards and procedures for making annual determinations of whether the earnings of each of the Class I railroads is sufficient to attract capital. This annual pass/fail appraisal of revenue adequacy has become ritualistic while offering little substantive information for regulators and policy makers in monitoring the industry's economic and competitive conditions.

The study committee recommends that STB discontinue issuing annual reports on the revenue adequacy of individual railroads and replace them with periodic studies of economic and competitive conditions in the industry.

Since the time that the TRB study was published, the most recent decision by the STB in a rate case (Consumers Energy) indicated a willingness by the Board to consider using the revenue adequacy standard in addition to or in place of the stand-alone-cost test going forward, a change which could add new relevance to the annual reports.

Strategic review of STB data programs with a focus on monitoring service quality

Until the Staggers Rail Act, all railroad traffic was moved in common carriage, and all rates and other terms of service were publicly posted and to a large degree similar. The Act made it possible for railroads to supply service by private contract, but retained the obligation of railroads to respond to requests for common carrier service for some types of traffic. Regulators, however, do not have reliable means to monitor the railroad response. The study argues that usable data on service quality be regularly collected in support of this monitoring function. In particular, shipment-specific data are needed

> to determine how the service provided in common carriage compares to that provided in contract carriage.
>
> Source: (TRB, 2015[41]), Modernizing Freight Rail Regulation, http://www.trb.org/Publications/Blurbs/172736.aspx. (accessed 1 May 2019); Consumers Energy v. CSX Transport, Surface Transportation Board, Decision, Docket No. NOR 42142, 11 January 2018, https://www.stb.gov/Decisions/readingroom.nsf/UNID/06AECC5B958B8C748525821200795A5A/$file/46230.pdf (accessed 4 June 2019).

Canadian regulation

Canadian regulation has a less clearly defined set of parameters for delimiting the circumstances in which tariffs can be regulated, but the governing concept is roughly the same as in the USA. Under the Canadian National Transportation Policy, competition and market forces, both within and among the various modes of transportation, are the prime agents for ensuring viable and effective transportation services. Regulation is used to achieve economic or social outcomes that cannot be achieved by competition and market forces alone. Policy aims to ensure that intervention does not unduly favour, or reduce the inherent advantages of any particular mode of transportation. Canadian regulatory remedies (inter-switching, final offer arbitration, level of service adjudication and arbitration) are available independently of the financial health of rail carriers and are fundamentally designed to provide shippers with additional leverage in their negotiations with railways or with more competitive rail options.

Canada does not use explicit numerical standards for revenue/cost ratios. It does collect detailed cost and revenue information, but does not make the information available to the public. Data filed with the Minister of Transport are held in confidence since the Canadian rail system is essentially a duopoly; each carrier could estimate the other's confidential information by simple subtraction from the total. The Canadian Transportation Agency (CTA) does require that the unit costs and costing manuals used in regulatory proceedings be approved by the CTA. Information on individual railways in similar circumstances in the USA is published, however, in the US Statistics of Class 1 Railroads.

The CTA relies much more heavily on alternative dispute resolution mechanisms (facilitation, mediation and arbitration) than the STB. The CTA has a broad range of alternative dispute resolution mechanisms including:

- Mediation, where an agency mediator helps parties resolve their differences through negotiation (face-to-face or by teleconference). Mediation is offered as an alternative to adjudication on any matter when both parties agree to pursue this approach.
- Final offer arbitration, where a shipper dissatisfied with the rates offered by a railway can ask that the dispute be arbitrated. Both the railway and the shipper must submit their final proposal along with justifying material. The arbitrator must consider whether the shipper has "an alternative, effective, adequate and competitive means of transporting the goods" as well as any other considerations believed to be relevant. The arbitrator must then choose between the two proposals and does not have to provide reasons for the decision, which is final and binding. This creates strong incentives for both shipper and railroad to make reasonable proposals, as the less reasonable the proposal the less likely to be adopted by the arbitrator.
- Final offer arbitration for rail level of service takes place where a shipper cannot agree on the terms of a service contract with the railway. The arbitrator is not limited in this instance to selecting either the offer of the railway or the shipper and can set its own conditions.

With the exception of the movement of western Canadian grain to certain destinations, where both Canadian National (CN) and Canadian Pacific (CP) are subject to a maximum revenue entitlement under the law (essentially by fixing an average rate per ton, adjusted by the volume of grain being moved), the CTA has limited power to impose rates.

The Canada Transportation Act offers three provisions to deal with the market power of railways by facilitating competitive access, namely: Regulated Inter-switching and Extended Inter-switching (sections 127-128); Competitive Line Rates (sections 129-136); and, Running Rights (section 138).

- The inter-switching provision has existed in law since the turn of the last century and is the only competitive access provision with any significant use. Under these provisions, a shipper has the right to require a railway to haul its traffic to a competing railway inter-switching point if the inter-switching point is less than 30 kilometres away (either at origin or destination or both). This movement is subject to rates prescribed by regulation, which must at least cover the variable costs of the movement. Recently, as a result of the bumper crop in Western Canada, this limit has been increased to 160 kilometres in the Prairies, a regime that could disappear two years after the coming into force of this new provision.
- The competitive line rate (CLR) was established in 1987 to allow a shipper to get two railways to move its traffic at a rate to be specified by the agency over distances greater than the inter-switching limits (CLR cannot be applied for more than 50% of the total distance or 1 200 kilometres, whichever is greater). This provision has had very limited use. The requirement for the competing connecting railway to formally agree to move the traffic of the captive shipper beyond the interchange to which the CLR is to be established is seen as a major roadblock.
- The running rights provision has been in place since 1967 and can be granted by the agency on a case-by-case basis. Running rights allow a federal railway to operate its trains and crews over the line(s) of another federal railway at a regulated rate, but not to solicit traffic along the rail lines of the host railway. There has, however, never been a successful application granting such rights by the agency. It should be noted that there are many examples of railways successfully negotiating running rights on a voluntary, commercial basis (e.g. the arrangement in the Vancouver area).

In addition, the CTA can establish the conditions, and rates to be paid, by public passenger service providers (via rail, urban transit authorities) for the use of railway facilities.

Interchange traffic

In both the US and Canada, if a railway cannot provide end-to-end service, an interchange of traffic with a railway (or railways) that serves the destination must take place if the shipment is to be made. In many cases, shippers or railroads have required interchanged traffic to be billed separately (so-called "Rule 11" rates) so that no railway has information about what the other is charging. In the event of a protest by a shipper, it would be possible for the STB to find that the total rate or any portion thereof is too high.

In the United States an essential condition of being a common carrier is that the railway must carry all traffic that is on offer on reasonable terms and that the railway must offer a reasonable tariff for doing so. If a railway cannot carry the traffic from origin to destination (estimates of the traffic interchanged among US railways range between 20 and 40%), then it must offer the shipper an opportunity to use a connection to another railway or railways, again on reasonable terms. If there is more than one routing possible, however, the shipper does not have the right to require a preferred route while, at the same time, demanding a lower tariff because this might severely complicate the route planning of all the railways involved. If the tariff offered is reasonable, that is sufficient. There can be limited exceptions to this rule if there are *"essential facilities"* involved and when the railway denies the use of the facilities or demands a price for use of the essential facilities that is unreasonably high.

In Canada, if the traffic is to move over a continuous route and portions of it are operated by two or more railway companies, the companies shall at the request of the shipper either agree on a joint tariff and the apportionment of the joint tariff, or enter into a confidential contract. If the railways cannot come to an agreement, a shipper may request that the CTA settle the matter. The agency has not had any such request in years, if ever.

References

AAR (2019), *Rail Traffic Data*, Association of American Railroads, Washington DC, https://www.aar.org/data-center/rail-traffic-data/ (accessed on 5 March 2019). [23]

ACCC (2014), *Tests for Assessing Cross-Subsidy*, Australian Competition & Consumer Commission, Canberra, https://www.accc.gov.au/system/files/Tests%20for%20assessing%20cross-subsidy_0_0.pdf (accessed on 2 March 2019). [37]

Algemene Rekenkamer (2016), *Exploitatie van de Betuweroute: Rapport Behorend bij Verantwoordingsonderzoek naar Begrotingshoofdstuk XII [Operation of the Betuwe route: Report Belonging to Accountability Investigation in Budget Chapter XII]*, Algemene Rekenkamer, The Hague, https://www.rekenkamer.nl/publicaties/rapporten/2016/05/18/exploitatie-van-de-betuweroute. [20]

Allen, R. (2001), *The Structure and Regulation of the Mexican Railroad Industry at the Beginning of the 21st Century*, Zuckert Scoutt & Rasenberg, L.L.P., https://www.zsrlaw.com/wp-content/uploads/sites/378/2016/05/Surface_Transportation_-_Allen_-_The_Structure_and_Regulation_of_the_Mexican_Railroad_Industry_2001.pdf (accessed on 2 March 2019). [6]

ARTF (2018), *Anuario Estadístico Ferroviario 2017 [Railway Statistical Yearbook 2017]*, SCT, https://www.gob.mx/artf/acciones-y-programas/anuario-estadistico-ferroviario-2017-152797. [12]

Bach, F. (1939), "The Nationalization of the Mexican Railroads", *Annals of the Public and Cooperative Economics*, Vol. 15/1, pp. 70-91, https://doi.org/10.1111/j.1467-8292.1939.tb00568.x. [2]

Baumol, W. (1987), *Direct Testimony. U.S. Postal Rate Commission Docket No. R87-1 (USPS-T-3)*. [36]

Boiteux, M. (1956), *Sur la gestion des Monopoles Publics astreints a l'equilibre budgetaire [The management of Public Monopolies constrained to a balanced budget]*, https://www.jstor.org/stable/pdf/1905256.pdf?refreqid=excelsior%3A390c3d0497baa6727d8c586ef1549b1e (accessed on 2 March 2019). [18]

COFECE (2016), *Reporte Preliminar sobre Competencia Efectiva en el Sistema Ferroviario Mexicano [Preliminar report on the Effective Competition in the Mexican Railway System]*. [4]

Decker, C. (2018), *Modern Economic Regulation. An Introduction to Theory and Practice*, Cambridge University Press, https://doi.org/10.1017/CBO9781139162500. [38]

Donly, A. (1920), "The Railroad Situation in Mexico", *The Journal of International Relations*, Vol. 11/2, pp. 234-251, https://www.jstor.org/stable/29738399 (accessed on 2 March 2019). [1]

Faulhaber, G. (1975), "Cross-Subsidization: Pricing in Public Enterprises", *The American Economic Review*, Vol. 65/5, pp. 966-977, https://www.jstor.org/stable/pdf/1806633.pdf?refreqid=excelsior%3Ab02eb762f9172a505823e6e700d4ad89 (accessed on 2 March 2019). [35]

Gobierno de Mexico (2018), *Modificación al Título de Asignación otorgado en favor de la empresa de participación estatal mayoritaria Ferrocarril del Istmo de Tehuantepec, S.A. de C.V. [Modification to the Allocation Title granted in favour of the majority state-owned joint venture*, DOF, CDMX, http://www.dof.gob.mx/nota_detalle.php?codigo=5514222&fecha=23/02/2018&print=true. [13]

Gobierno de Mexico (2017), *Modificación al Título de Concesión otorgado en favor de Ferrocarril Pacífico-Norte, S.A. de C.V., hoy Ferrocarril Mexicano, S.A. de C.V. [Modification to the Title of Concession granted in favour of Ferrocarril Pacífico-Norte, S.A. de C.V., today Ferroca*, DOF, CDMX, http://dof.gob.mx/nota_detalle.php?codigo=5234598&fecha=21/02/2012. [14]

Gobierno de Mexico (1997), *Concesión otorgada en favor de Ferrocarril Pacífico-Norte, S.A. de C.V., respecto de la Vía corta Ojinaga-Topolobampo.[Concession granted in favor of Ferrocarril Pacífico-Norte, S.A. de C.V., with respect to the Short Vía Ojinaga-Topolobampo]*, DOF, CDMX, http://www.dof.gob.mx/nota_detalle.php?codigo=4903433&fecha=11/12/1997CONCESION otorgada en favor de Ferrocarril Pacífico-Norte, S.A. de C.V., respecto de la Vía corta Ojinaga-Topolobampo. [15]

Gobierno de Mexico (1996), *Acuerdo mediante el cual se destina al servicio de la SCT los inmbuebles de la vía general de comunicación ferroviaria del Noreste, así como de los que prestan los servicios auxiliares, con objeto de que esa Dependencia otorgue sobre dichos inmuebles las concesiones y permisos respectivos [Agreement by means of which all properties of the Northeast route and for rendering auxiliary services are destined to the SCT]*, DOF, CDMX, http://www.dof.gob.mx/nota_detalle.php?codigo=4906174&fecha=29/11/1996. [7]

Gobierno de México (1995), *Acuerdo por el que se crea la Comisión Intersecretarial de Desincorporación [Agreement establishing the Intersecretarial De-incorporation Commission]*, DOF, CDMX, http://dof.gob.mx/nota_detalle.php?codigo=4872087&fecha=07/04/1995 (accessed on 2 March 2019). [3]

Huneke, W. (2017), "The Political Economy of Regulatory Costing: The Development of the Uniform Rail Costing System", *Journal of Transportation Law, Logistics and Policy*, Vol. 84/2, pp. 196-223, http://www.atlp.org/journal.html. [29]

ICC (1985), *Coal Rate Guidelines, Nationwide*. [33]

ITF (2018), *ITF Transport Statistics-Goods Transport*, http://dx.doi.org/10.1787/trsprt-data-en. [25]

ITF (2014), *Freight Railway Development in Mexico*, OECD Publishing, Paris, https://dx.doi.org/10.1787/5jlwvzjd60kb-en. [8]

ITF (2014), "Freight Railway Development in Mexico", *International Transport Forum Policy Papers*, No. 1, OECD Publishing, Paris, https://dx.doi.org/10.1787/5jlwvzjd60kb-en. [16]

Kahn, A. (1971), *The Economics of Regulation: Principles and Institutions*, John Wiley and Sons. [39]

Mac Donald, J. (1989), "Railroad Deregulation, Innovation, and Competition: Effects of the Staggers Act on Grain", *The Journal of Law & Economics*, Vol. 32/1, pp. 63-95. [31]

Mac Donald, J. (1987), "Competition and Rail Rates for the Shipment of Corn", *The RAND Journal of Economics*, Vol. 18/1, pp. 151-163. [32]

McCullough, G. (2008), *Statement before the Surface Transportation Board on URCS costing*. [28]

Middleton, W., G. Smerk and R. Diehl (2007), "Mexican Railroads General History", *Encyclopedia of American Railways*. [10]

ORR (2018), *2018 Periodic Review: ORR's Draft Determination-Summary of Conclusions England & Wales*, ORR, London, https://orr.gov.uk/__data/assets/pdf_file/0006/27789/pr18-draft-determination-executive-summary-england-and-wales.pdf (accessed on 2 March 2019). [21]

ORR (2013), *Periodic Review 2013*, ORR, London, http://orr.gov.uk/rail/economic-regulation/regulation-of-network-rail/price-controls/periodic-review-2013/pr13-guide/about-pr13. [22]

Pittman, R. (2017), "The Srange Career of Independent Voting Trusts in U.S, Rail Mergers", *Journal of Competition Law & Econmics*, Vol. 13/1, pp. 89-102. [19]

Pittman, R. (2016), *Remarks before the STB Economic Roundtable Discussion: Issues, Conclusions of Independent Study on Railroad Rate-Case Methodologies*, Washington DC, https://www.stb.gov/stb/audiomee.nsf/71c35e25bd34f1f68525653300425877/a8f449222a9cca5185258059005061a5?OpenDocument. [43]

Pittman, R. (2010), "Against the Stand-Alone-Cost Test in U.S. Freight Rail Regulation", *Journal of Regulatory Economics*, Vol. 38/3, pp. 313-326, https://link.springer.com/content/pdf/10.1007%2Fs11149-010-9130-3.pdf (accessed on 2 March 2019). [40]

Pittman, R. (2010), "The Economics of Railroad "Captive Shipper" Legislation", US Department of Justice, http://www.usdoj.gov/atr/public/eag/discussionpapers.htm. (accessed on 2 March 2019). [42]

RAC (2013), *2014 Rail Trends*, Railway Association of Canada, Ottawa, https://www.railcan.ca/wp-content/uploads/2016/10/2014_RAC_RailTrends.pdf (accessed on 5 March 2019). [24]

Railway Gazette (1997), *TFM wins Noreste concession*, https://www.railwaygazette.com/news/single-view/view/tfm-wins-noreste-concession.html. [9]

Ramsey, F. (1927), *A Contribution to the Theory of Taxation*, https://www.jstor.org/stable/pdf/2222721.pdf?refreqid=excelsior%3Ab3574348888b93a69e08e33153207f17 (accessed on 2 March 2019). [17]

SCT (2015), *Anuario Estadístico Sector Comunicaciones y Transportes 2014 [2014 Statistical Yearbook of the Communications and Transport Sector]*, Secretaría de Comunicaciones y Transportes, CDMX, http://www.sct.gob.mx/fileadmin/DireccionesGrales/DGP/estadistica/Anuarios/Anuario_2014.pdf. [11]

SCT (1997), *Concesión que otorga el Gobierno Federal, por conducto de la Secretaría de Comunicaciones y Transportes, en favor de Ferrocarril del Noreste, S.A. de C.V. [Concession granted by the Federal Government, through the Secretariat of Communications and Transport, in favour of Ferrocarril del Noreste, S.A. de C.V.]*, http://www.dof.gob.mx/nota_detalle.php?codigo=4866123&fecha=03/02/1997 (accessed on 2 March 2019). [5]

Secretaría de Comunicaciones y Transporte (2014), *Anuario Estadístico, Sector Comunicaciones y Transporte 2013 [2013 Statistical Yearbook, Communications and Transport Sector]*, DOF, CDMX, http://www.sct.gob.mx/fileadmin/DireccionesGrales/DGP/estadistica/Anuarios/Anuario-2013.pdf. [27]

STB (2019), *Carload Waybill Sample*, https://www.stb.gov/stb/industry/econ_waybill.html (accessed on 6 March 2019). [30]

STB (2018), *Statistics of Class 1 Freight Railroads*, Surface Transportation Board, Washington DC, https://www.stb.gov/Econdata.nsf/M%20Statistics%20of%20Class%201%20Feight%20RR?OpenPage (accessed on 5 March 2019). [26]

STB (2006), *Major Issues in Rail Rate Cases*, Surface Transportation Board, Washington DC, https://www.stb.gov/decisions/readingroom.nsf/UNID/5C7E822CBDC68AD385257217005C5064/$file/37406.pdf (accessed on 2 March 2019). [34]

TRB (2015), *Modernizing Freight Rail Regulation*, TRB Publications, http://www.trb.org/Publications/Blurbs/172736.aspx. [41]

Wilson, W. and F. Wolak (2016), "Freight Rail Costing and Regulation: The Uniform Rail Costing System", *Review of Industrial Organization*, Vol. 49/2, pp. 229-261, http://dx.doi.org/10.1007/s11151-016-9523-2. [44]

4 Internal governance of the Regulatory Agency for Rail Transport

The section briefly explains the seven OECD Best Practice Principles of the Governance of Regulators, which aim at improving the performance of regulatory agencies. For each principle under consideration, it describes the institutional arrangements and practices of the ARTF comparted with each principle.

The current section is mainly based on the Best Practice of the Governance of Regulators (OECD, 2014[1]). The objective of the principles is to establish an effective regulatory policy which comprises "a consistent policy covering the role of functions of regulatory agencies in order to provide greater confidence that regulatory decisions are made on an objective, impartial and consistent basis, without conflict of interest, bias or improper influence" (OECD, 2012[2]). The seven principles are the following and will be described in detail in this section:

- Role clarity
- Preventing undue influence and maintaining trust
- Decision-making and governing body structure for independent regulators
- Accountability and transparency
- Engagement
- Funding
- Performance evaluation

Role clarity

The basic idea of the *role clarity* principle is that an effective regulator must have clear objectives and clear functions, embedded in a complete regulatory framework and other policy instruments. These functions shall be sufficient enough to accomplish the institutional objectives that gave origin to the regulators' creation. This principle's main justification: only through clear objectives and statements can the institution achieve the expected results and goals.

These regulators' objectives should not be in conflict or competing with goals; they can otherwise undermine institutional performance. Only when clear benefits surpass potential costs should they be joined. However, in a situation where a regulator combines competing objectives, a regulatory framework and guidelines must be developed to help the institution trade off such functions. On the other hand, within the institution, these objectives should reflect separate and specific functions, goals, budget, personnel, etc. Therefore, a multi-purpose regulator would face important challenges in planning and executing all responsibilities and functions.

The legal framework should indicate the co-ordination mechanisms by which the regulator must co-operate with other institutions, such as congress, ministries, autonomous bodies, etcetera, on topics of shared responsibility. On the other hand, any co-operation agreement, memorandum of understanding or formal agreement should be published on the regulators' websites to promote transparency in the roles of the regulator.

Finally, clear separation of functions and co-ordination with ministries is a relevant issue. The role of the regulators with regard to supporting the policy objectives of ministries can vary across countries. A common practice, however, is the independence principle of regulators, which would limit the responsibility to supporting ministries on policy issues. Notwithstanding, support on policy issues is a fact and regulators' involvement in different stages of policy formulation is also desirable as co-ordination between promotion and regulation reduces uncertainty and misleading expectations over the role of regulated entities.

The objectives and functions of the ARTF are scattered in several legal documents. The Decree SCT-26-01-2015 ordering the creation of the agency was published on January 26, 2015 in the Official Gazette. This legal instrument establishes the basic attributions of the ARTF and the SCT regarding the regulation and promotion of the rail sector. For instance, the SCT has the objective of planning and developing the public policy of the rail services, as well as regulating its development. On the other hand, the agency is in charge of several regulatory duties.

The ARTF, however, was created as a deconcentrated body of the SCT until August 18, 2016. The agency was granted with technical, operational and administrative capacity. The Decree SCT-18-08-2016 states additional operative and regulatory functions to those established in the Decree 26-01-2015. The former reinforces the both types of attributions of the agency, regulation and promotion of the rail sector.

The Law on the Regulation of Rail Services was reformed in 2015 and 2016, through which changes to the legal framework of the rail sector took place. Additionally, in 2017, the law was amended to include the current attributions of the agency, and in 2018 further changes on tariffs regulation were included. Notwithstanding, the regulatory framework of the agency is not complete and operational matters are yet to be defined more clearly. For example, some attributions of the ARTF are carried out by the General Direction of Rail and Multimodal Transport Development (DGDFM), and vice versa; and some attributions may not be carried out at all.

Table 4.1 includes a selection of the regulatory and non-regulatory duties of the ARTF according to the legal framework. The agency faces competing objectives regarding its regulatory role in the rail sector and the promotion and expansion of the system. In principle, the promotion of the industry is mainly carried out by the Ministry of Transport and Communications, through the DGDFM. Ideally, the ARTF should not have any promotion activities, as it implies an overlap of functions and it may create opposite incentives, as promotion and regulatory duties may clash with each other.

Table 4.1. Selected functions of the ARTF

Law on the Regulation of Rail Services

Regulatory functions	Non-regulatory functions
Define technical standards of the rail transport and infrastructure and verify its compliance	Promote the expansion and use of the rail network; and identify the short lines underused to take them back under state control
Guarantee interconnection services and determine interconnection tariffs in cases where agreements cannot be reached	Provide recommendations on security issues
Determine the tariffs and regulatory bases if there is lack of competition	Elaborate and publish statistical records and indicators for rail services
Impose fines and sanctions due to non-compliance of the obligations established on the concession titles and other regulations	

Source: Adapted from the Law on the Regulation of Rail Services.

As seen in Table 4.1 the ARTF has the task to promote the use of the rail network and identify underused lines. The usage of the network may be promoted through regulatory functions, but encouraging the expansion of the network may imply the handout of incentives, such as regulatory moratoriums, that may be opposite to the regulatory duties. Furthermore, the Law does not establish a hierarchy of duties.

A fundamental part of the role of a regulatory agency is to have the necessary resources to discharge its functions effectively. When the ARTF was created and its roles defined, some gaps in terms of organisational structure and regulatory framework were left unattended, which are likely to undermine the performance of the agency. This includes limitations to carry out inspections, gaps in regulation to carry out sanction duties, and lack of sufficient staff and personnel.

One of the issues arises with the lack of installed capacity for ARTF to carry out inspections. The ARTF has an annual inspection programme which aims at inspecting the entirety of the railroads with an operational prioritisation following the accidents of previous years – the 2018 programme established 909 inspections as a goal. However, the creation of the decentralised Agency was not accompanied by a formal structure to effectively enforce the law. When the regulatory functions were part of the SCT, the inspections and data gathering across the country were made through the SCT Centres – the SCT Centres are the local representatives of the SCT across Mexico.

The creation of the ARTF as a decentralised body reduced its actual capacity to inspect in Mexican states, as the SCT Centres still belong to the ministry. Nowadays the SCT centres support the ARTF; however, this co-ordination is not made through formal agreements. This lack of formalisation can create tensions in the effectiveness of the inspection process to meet the agency's standards.

Another issue has to do with sanctions and fines. Currently, the ARTF does not have specific guidelines about imposing fines and sanctions, making it harder to effectively sanction regulated parties.

The final issue is related to the endowment of sufficient personnel. During the elaboration of this review, the ARTF did not have enough personnel to accomplish its duties – 18 officials in total. One of the causes of this situation is that the DGDFM has not yet transferred the remaining staff with regulatory powers to the agency – 49 officials. Due to these circumstances, there was an overlap in functions, personnel and roles between the staff of both agencies. It is worth mentioning that the transferring of personnel follows an administrative procedure that goes beyond the scope of the SCT and involves the participation of the Ministry of Finance (SHCP) and the Ministry of Public Administration (SFP).

Preventing undue influence and maintaining trust

The notion of the principle is that regulators need to instil trust between stakeholders and institutions. In order to build this trust, close communication must be maintained with regulated entities and other parties; at the same time, the regulator must avoid any undue influence that may lead to regulatory capture.

The work of the regulators must be grounded in objectivity and impartiality. Thus, if there is a situation in which the scope of the regulator covers government and non-government firms, competitive neutrality is required to avoid distrust and reduce the risk of undue influence by public firms.

Formal and situation independence can promote objectivity and impartiality. Legal statutes can grant legal independence of regulators while independence can arise from institutional strength or the implementation of better practices. Both schemes face advantages and challenges. The choice between the two depends on several conditions, for example, the need to demonstrate independence, the dynamics of policy at the national level, the institutional strength of the country, etc.

Undue influence can arise from any governmental institution (ministries, congress, the executive, autonomous bodies, judiciary power, etc.), regulated entities or the public. The regulator must interact with these parties to deploy the regulatory process, co-ordinating on issues of shared responsibilities, consulting over regulatory projects and receiving feedback about the strategy and instruments it applies. Within this interaction, however, the regulator must pursue the institutional objective in the short and the long term, avoiding undue influence.

Avoiding regulatory capture and maintaining trust ensures that regulators, in fact, pursue their underlying policy objectives. There are several practices, which contribute to reduce the risk of regulatory capture and therefore create trust. For instance; the "revolving doors" restriction for officials working in regulated firms after certain periods of time; transparent communication between regulators and stakeholders; a defined agenda and official channels of communication; the degree of formal and legal independence; the implementation of regulatory impact assessment (RIA) and the consultation process for regulatory production; the selection process and the terms of the board members, etc. Principles such as the governing body of the regulator, the degree of independence, the fundraising scheme, the accountability obligations and the evaluation of the performance, also help limit the risk of regulatory capture.

Regulators can range from ministerial to autonomous bodies. Challenges linked to undue influence and trust are different in both situations. In principle, influence may be more probable between ministerial regulators in comparison with governing bodies, but the former may face challenges in a timely and effective manner. The election between a regulator within a ministry or an autonomous body is dependent on institutional arrangements and institutional capacity, not only linked to the regulator but also public entities.

During the drafting of the report, the ARTF did not have yet an explicit cross-sectional strategy to prevent undue influence, as its first efforts focused on other priorities. For example, the assurance of financial and human resources to reach its duties. In contrast, the ARTF has scattered practices inherited from the previous organisation as a general direction under the umbrella of the SCT. Some of these practices focus on the institutional communications with the stakeholders:

- Regarding the regulated entities, the ARTF holds public and monthly case-by-case meetings with the AMF and representatives of the concessions holders. Besides, the agency meets with rail firms in response to specific problematics (e.g. vandalism, accidents, etc.).
- The relation with other public institutions is also conducted on a case-by-case scenario. For instance, the interaction with COFECE relies on potential cases of competition in the rail industry – at the time of drafting this Review, the COFECE was carrying out a second study to determine the existence of monopolistic behaviour in the rail sector. On the other hand, the institutional co-ordination with CONAMER focuses on the regulatory quality process, mainly through the implementation of the RIA for draft regulations – which includes the consultation process. Now, most of the discussion with CONAMER focuses on the accomplishment of the one-in, one-out rule, which requires the elimination of administrative burdens equal to that imposed by the new regulation. The ARTF also co-ordinates with SCT, through the General Direction of Preventive Medicine and the DGDFM. With the former, the agency works to issue the licences of the rail crews, which includes a medical examination. Regarding its relation to the DGDFM, the ARTF implements the obligations included in the concession titles and in the regulatory framework. With the later, the creation process of the ARTF has extended the efficient and effective co-ordination in practice; officials of both institutions and responsibilities are still mixed up.
- There is no evidence of systematic practices of interaction between the agency and the public.

Transparency and accountability are strong tools to ensure trust. The ARTF complies with the legal obligations established in the general framework of the Mexican government. However, independence demands more efforts on transparency and accountability.

Finally, the ARTF has revolving door limits as officials cannot work for one year in the industry, after the end of its appointment period.

Decision making and government body structure for independent regulators

The design of the governing body and the decision-making powers have an impact on the effectiveness of the regulators, the delivery of the regulatory policy and expected results of institutional objectives. Additionally, the governing body has an influence on the regulators' integrity as it can affect the risk of regulatory capture.

The governing body of the regulator can take different forms:

- The governance board model: oversight, strategic guidance and operational policy.
- The commission model: a board advises on regulatory decisions.
- The single member model: one individual takes the regulatory decisions.

The selection of the model *per se* has some effects on the effectiveness of the regulator. For instance, under certain conditions, a commission or a governance board model reduces the risk of regulatory capture and strengthens the decision-making in comparison with the single member model.

Membership to the governing body is an important institutional arrangement that would go against regulatory capture and promote transparency. In order to go in this direction, the policies, criteria and selection process of the terms of appointment must be transparent. Government body members can be elected by public opposition contest or by direct appointment from an authority. Public opposition contest, however, creates greater trust if carried out fairly and inclusively.

Direct election of the board is another common practice of regulators. A single authority or different public officials can elect this type of governing body. The model requires, however, more transparency in the selection criteria as there could be bias in the process. For example, stakeholders, industry and ministry representation can be in conflict with the need to have board members with a technical background. Regulators must follow their institutional objectives but members can be influenced or have a biased opinion due to their public position. Thus, clear statements over objectives and goals, as well as guidelines to reduce conflict are advisable.

A multi-member model also has more institutional memory when the replacement is staggered. Due to this reason, changes in the board are less costly and less likely to modify the work of the regulator completely. This model can remove the institution from the political process. For instance, the appointment of board members can go beyond the period of the elected government in place.

In general and regardless of the governing model, corporate models have accommodating features to enhance the regulators' accountability, transparency, effectiveness, integrity and independence. In contrast, a single member can be more adaptable to industry changes and more responsive. Regulatory capture is more challenging with a single member but institutional strength of the head ministry can be of support in this matter.

According to the Article 4 of the ARTF's creation decree, the governing body relies in a single official, which is the head of the agency. The president appoints and removes the head by recommendation of the SCT without a defined period. Moreover, there are neither clear selection criteria nor well-defined professional profiles for the person in charge of the agency. Finally, there is not a public tender for applicants to the position. The selection process together with scattered practices to create trust may increase the risk of undue influence and the appointment of unfitted profiles.

The head is the maximum authority of the ARTF. It has both, administrative and policy-making functions. Thus, the head proposes and executes the annual budget, negotiates inter-institutional agreements. Besides, the head is the main responsible to implement rail regulation and to suggest draft regulations.

The governing body for an independent regulator should fulfil certain requirements:

- Set specific appointment periods in legal instruments, ideally in a primary law;
- Define the professional profiles of the candidates;
- Define early removal criteria and processes for the member(s) of the body;
- Establish an open public tender that takes into account relevant characteristics, such as technical profiles, experience and examinations results. The tender should be conducted by an unbiased evaluation committee;
- In the case of a board, the appointments should be stepped and ensure a complete quorum. If possible, the board should be separated from the technical areas of the agency.

The decision-making body of the regulator can be comprised by a single head or by a board. Regardless of the governing model, in general terms, corporate models have features more accommodating to enhance accountability, transparency, effectiveness, integrity and independence of the regulator. In contrast, single member decision-making bodies can be more adaptable to industry changes and the responsiveness can be faster. In contrast, regulatory capture is more challenging when there is a single member but institutional strength of the head ministry can support on this matter.

At the same time, single heads of regulators are more fitted when the institutional arrangements of the public system are stronger and favour independence. Besides, a board is more effective when there is a necessity to show independence in the decision making process.

Accountability and transparency

This principle highlights the relevance of accountability and transparency for economic regulators. In fact, accountability and transparency are the foundations of trust but also a mechanism to align expectations between regulators and stakeholders. The main message of the principle is that compulsory or self-imposed practices in accountability and transparency promote the decision-making process and provide elements to lower the risk of regulatory capture.

Governments usually keep transparency and accountability obligations for all public entities, including the regulators. Notwithstanding, independent regulators should go beyond these duties in comparison with all public entities; thus, as long as regulators advance on independence or autonomy, they should increase their accountability and transparency practices to strengthen trust.

Accountability obligations could include the executive, congress, the public and stakeholders. Of course, the areas to be accountable for are not necessarily the same for all the stakeholders. For instance, the executive may focus on policy objectives, co-ordination with ministries and budget execution; congress would focus on policy objectives and budget execution; and the public and stakeholders may focus on policy objectives. In these topics, it is relevant that regulators publish their operational plans for each year, so the stakeholders can compare the planned agenda with the achieved results.

In perspective, transparency is a sort of accountability for the public and the value of the information published is worth the additional work involved. Thus, regulators should publish all possible information about their operation, including budget execution, industry statistics, annual working plans, meetings with stakeholders and their summaries, goals and objectives achieved, etc. This information should be readily accessible for most potential users and in manageable formats. It is also advisable that regulators pay attention to the information needed by users and include it in day-to-day statistics. Regulators should follow a transparency policy as a mechanism to obtain trust.

Regarding transparency obligations and accountability, the ARTF is subject to the same regulations as any public institution in Mexico. For instance, the officials' contact information, salaries, profiles, functions, etc. are available to the public through web portals. In terms of financial information, the agency publishes its budget plans and execution.

Currently, the ARTF – as a deconcentrated body – is accountable to the SCT and to the SHCP. However, it is not directly accountable to the Congress.

The ARTF publishes statistical information of the rail industry (tariffs, tonne-km, routes, accidents and vandalism, amongst others), mainly through a yearbook or quarterly reports. Nonetheless, this information is neither exhaustive nor detailed and it is not published in handily formats. The main sources of information are the railway firms, which submit part of the data as the agency requests it and not following a standardised calendar, formats or processes. As a result, several areas of the SCT may ask for the same information more than once. At the moment of this Review, the ARTF mentioned that it is building up a digital platform to collect and publish statistical information.

Stakeholder engagement

The engagement principle refers to an integral policy of interacting with regulated entities and other stakeholders. The relevance of engaging with stakeholders is down to the fact that regulators learn from the industry how it works; from the public the effects of regulation; and from public entities how to work together.

Engagement with stakeholders is also a mechanism to produce quality regulation as they can provide feedback about a specific problem and proposals to solve them. Through engagement activities, regulators can improve the relationship with stakeholders, as they can offer opinions about potential problems and the effects of regulation as well as anticipate regulation and reduce implementation costs and uncertainty.

It is important that regulators commit to a policy on stakeholder engagement. Most regulators have active contact with their regulated firms and other actors but this is slightly different from a policy approach. A policy on stakeholder engagement requires objectives, a scheduled and planned agenda to discuss regulatory issues, analysis of the discussion topics, etc.

Engagement undertakings are highly recommended but regulators must take into account best practices in such activities to avoid risks of regulatory capture and conflict of interest. At the same time, regulators must be clear on the purpose of these activities, so the stakeholders fulfil their expectations. Finally, all exercises should fit the purpose; this means that activities need rationality criteria. For example, it may be excessive to undertake a complex, expensive and full consultation *in situ* for a proposed small regulation with few expected potential effects. Thus, consultation practices as early consultation, regulatory impact assessment and *ex post* consultation (under *ex post* evaluation activities) should be adopted as part of the engagement policy.

The main contact points between the ARTF and its stakeholders are the programmed meetings and the consultation process during the draft of regulations, which is managed by CONAMER. As mentioned above, there is not a systematic planning of the meetings and the relevant topics to be addressed by the sector. Since the ARTF does not have a regulatory stock to comply with the one-in one-out rule which limits its capacity to issue regulation, the participation of relevant stakeholders in the drafting of rail regulation has been limited.

Another channel for the engagement with stakeholders is the early consultation process. Its main objective is to identify potential problems and alternatives before creating a draft regulation. Currently, there is no evidence about the systematic use of this practice.

Funding

The principle has at least two branches. In the first place, funding is the channel that allows the regulator to achieve the goals according to objectives. On the other hand, funding sources can contribute to ensuring independence (mainly from the government but also from the regulated firms) in the decision-making process and the implementation of the regulation.

The number of funding sources available for the regulators must be objectives-planned and set with goals in mind. The funding for regulators must be sufficient to achieve the expected goals in the given timeline – which can include yearly or longer aims. In fact, the planning of goals and budget is closely aligned. Still, the budget should not be the main driver, as sometimes a tight budget is assigned to accomplish high goals. This does not otherwise mean that regulators should be granted substantial budgets. More than that, there must be a balance between budget and goals and the key is planning.

Sources of funding and easy access to funds are also a relevant issue for independence purposes. Independence relies on institutional arrangements between the regulators and the entities responsible for providing funding. These arrangements could be strong and it may not be necessary to separate the regulators' budget from other institutions, as is the case when the agency is part of a ministry or the former validates the budget. If the arrangements are strong over time, it is possible to maintain such structure but, if there is a perceived risk of change in policy, it may be sensible to separate the budget from the ministry through legal instruments. Assigning legal powers to the regulator to evaluate, propose, and implement the budget, helps to reduce the risk of capture and alleviate potential pressures to influence the regulator's decisions. Particular arrangements about the budget depend on country profiles and institutional capacity, but it is worth mentioning that self-budget planning and execution works towards independence.

The creation decree of the ARTF in 2016 did not grant the agency with the necessary financial resources for its operation nor established a source of funding that ensures the compliance of its objectives. The transfer of regulatory obligations from the SCT to the ARTF was restricted by the impossibility of increasing the SCT's budget at the time. This division implies an operational challenge, as the legal and managerial issues were addressed by the SCT. Currently, the agency requires administrative staff, which creates an extra burden on the budget.

According to the ARTF, the agency lacks human resources with technical skills, but the current budget limits the possibility of devoting resources to hiring additional personnel. Furthermore, the agency cannot conduct a proper inspections policy, as it does not have the necessary financial and human inputs. In order for the ARTF to follow a results-based approach, it must have enough resources and independency to allocate them.

The ARTF requires a stable and sufficient budget. Nowadays, in order to get resources, the agency negotiates with the SCT – meaning that the agency submits a proposal to the Ministry and the former decides whether it agrees or not. Most of the times there is a reduction in the budget presented by the ARTF, as the Ministry has to negotiate (with the SHCP) a general budget for the sector.

The ideal arrangement of the ARTF's funding scheme implies a direct transfer of the existing fee that regulated entities must pay to the government (2% of their income) – which now goes to the Federal budget. The agency must manage its own resources according to its needs. An additional measure is that the ARTF negotiates its budget directly with the SHCP.

It is worth mentioning that the agency should not receive the resources collected through fines, as it creates incentives to sanction when there is no need.

Performance evaluation

This principle encourages regulators to conduct performance evaluation according to the underlying policy objectives. If the regulator does not evaluate its work and actions, it will never know if the effects of its intervention are in line with their objectives and if there has been a return on invested resources.

Performance evaluation allows regulators to strengthen the activities or actions that contribute the most to their goals and modify those with poor effects. Due to the relevance of the performance evaluation, it is important to conduct these exercises periodically. The frequency depends on the relevance of the policy and the type of evaluation. For instance, an evaluation of performance indicators regarding outcomes can be launched on a yearly basis, as they need "simple" statistical analysis, which is not as time-consuming. On the other hand, the actual impact or effects of the regulatory decisions require analysis that is more complex and advanced tools. At the same time, identification of the final effects may be blurred in the early stages of implementation.

Finally, the publication of the results is as important as the launch of performance evaluation activities. It helps with accountability and transparency issues.

According to the ARTF, it is working on the creation of the National System of Rail Indicators, which will include information of the sector. However, at the time of this Review, there is no information on the status or possible release date of the system.

Currently the agency does not have performance indicators to assess the effectiveness of its regulatory policy.

References

OECD (2014), *OECD Best Practice Principles for Regulatory Policy*, OECD Publishing, Paris, https://doi.org/10.1787/23116013. [1]

OECD (2012), *Recommendation of the Council on Regulatory Policy and Governance*, OECD Publishing, Paris, https://dx.doi.org/10.1787/9789264209022-en. [2]

Glossary and definitions

Access rights	Rights to use railway infrastructure with the purpose of granting a company the possibility of operating trains.
Bypass	It is a new rail line that replaces or complements an existing one. Bypasses may be built to avoid difficult crossings, a city, a built-up area, town, etc.
Freight yards	Areas where freight cargo is managed, as it is loaded and unloaded from the trains.
Haulage rights	An agreement where one railroad company carries traffic on its line and on its trains on behalf of another company. The owner of the line receives a fee for providing access to the other company. The main distinction between haulage and trackage rights is the company who operates the trains.
Interchange traffic	Freight cargo that is exchanged from one railroad to another.
Interline traffic	Traffic that originates on one concessionary and terminates on another concessionary. An interline move involves more than one concessionary.
Rail gauges	The minimum perpendicular distance between the inner faces of two rails.
Slots	It is the capacity of a company to use its trains on a specific stretch of track during a given period of time.
Trackage rights	An agreement under which a tenant railroad gets rights from the owner of the track's rights to provide transportation service over the joint facility and it is the sole responsible for loss or damage of the freight. The tenant pays a fee to compensate the owner for track maintenance, train dispatching, among other expenses.
Trunk lines	Main supply channels, usually handle long-distance traffic.

www.ingramcontent.com/pod-product-compliance
Lightning Source LLC
LaVergne TN
LVHW061943070526
838199LV00060B/3940